HOOKED!

HOOKED!

Fishing Memories

George Melly

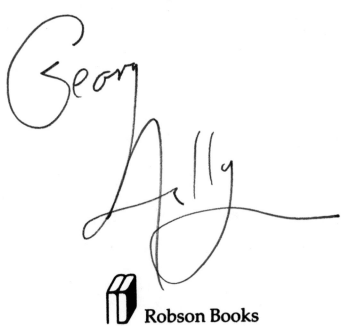

Robson Books

For Diana who always made sure I'd somewhere to cast, and Tom who threaded on that first worm.

First published in Great Britain in 2000 by Robson Books, 10 Blenheim Court, Brewery Road, London N7 9NT

A member of the Chrysalis Group plc

British Library Cataloguing in Publication Data
A catalogue record for this title is available from the British Library

ISBN 1 86105 275 8

Typeset by SX Composing DTP, Rayleigh, Essex
Printed in Great Britain by Butler & Tanner, London and Frome.

CONTENTS

INTRODUCTION

Tell your stories of fishing and other men's wives,
The expansive moments of restricted lives
In the lighted inn . . .

W. H. Auden

How have I the *chutzpa* to add a book on fishing to the already groaning shelves? Books instructional, theoretical, reminiscent, lyrical, modest, ego-boosting, radical, snobbish, beautifully written, comic and poetic.

No one will learn much from these pages on a practical level. I take it for granted that most, if not all of, my potential readers already fish. I have to my knowledge made only three converts in my whole life and a convert is anyway in my view only a fisherman who hasn't yet recognised that he is one. The first was the jazz clarinet player and, later, journalist, Ian Christie, who caught the bug from me on our long tour of the Scottish borders in the Fifties; the second, Ricky, a rock-drummer and composer, born in California, and of Goan ancestry, Mr Laidback himself, who was instantly adept, and soon became much more expert than I ever was or will be. The third was a columnist on the *Guardian*, who heard a broadcast by me on the subject and felt impelled to put my claims to the test. On a stocked reservoir in Barnes he caught his first rainbow trout and wrote a piece about it, more or less cursing me for adding a further complication to his life. Hardly a miraculous draft of fishers!

I know, in fact, only too well that to mention an interest in fishing to anyone who is neither an angler, nor, more rarely, a potential angler, is to watch their eyes cloud over with instant mental cataracts. At the same time they manage to imply that *not* fishing is somehow a share in their moral portfolio. In masking their aggression they tend more often than not to rely on a seemingly self-deprecating dismissal. It is, and I couldn't begin to counter the times I've heard it, 'I haven't got the patience.'

I have learnt to acknowledge that this is a signal to change the conversation. When I was young I believed that anything which aroused my enthusiasm must, if rightly presented, convince others, whether it was the Blues of Bessie Smith, the paintings of Max Ernst, the theory of Anarchism or of course, and indeed especially, fishing. For whom, then, do I write, for whom retrace my footsteps down those memory lanes that lead to waters both past and present, containing, or believing to contain, fish?

Well I have read, and suppose believe, although it seems incredible, that there are more people who fish than watch football matches. This statistic, if it's true, is well concealed by the fact that anglers never assemble in huge numbers, that while occasional sinners are brought to book (using maggots on fly-only waters, seeding a run with fish-farm pellets to start a feeding frenzy) there is no equivalent of football hooliganism, no post-match pissing down people's areas, shouting of racial or religious insults or the regurgitation of take-away tandooris in the streets. Of course, the serious football fan deplores these yobbish manifestations as much as anyone, but the point is that wherever he brings *his* passion up he will instantly set off a lively and vigorous debate. Those indifferent, as I am, to this national obsession simply remain silent.

Fishing, though, is a different matter, despite the weekly and monthly magazines at several levels, despite the comparatively generous series on television. If I write for anyone it is the silent majority; those for whom the supreme thrill, especially after hours of inactivity, is when the rod bends, the line screams off the reel, the hook holds and, after a tension-filled fight, the fish surfaces, turns over on his side and the net slides under him. To see him safely grassed is to give rise, even as you either kill him or return him to the water, to an almost post-orgasmic sensation. Indeed I read of an old Scottish gentleman, a virgin, who said that, from what he'd heard, having a woman must be not unlike playing and landing a 'fish' (Scots for a salmon).

While no virgin, I am, as the years clock up, more and more

inclined to agree with him. I can even offer proof, and I wonder if this incident, which I have never admitted before, strikes a chord in others. Over twenty years ago, when I was in my early fifties, I'd hooked and grassed a large trout on the River Usk in Wales. I was wading at the time down the side of a long but narrow island, impenetrable in summer because of its chest-high weeds. On impulse, the dead trout in one hand and using the closed net as a kind of machete, I carved a path through this mini rain forest until I'd found a small clearing. There I laid the beautifully marked fish on a tree stump as if it were a sacrifice, and lying down where I could see it (a ludicrous sight, no doubt, in my thigh-waders) masturbated into a large dock leaf. I have never succeeded in pinning down my solitary and unique motivation, although it would seem to confirm the supposition of the old and virginal Scottish gentleman but, this one episode apart, sex from now on will play little part in these pages. There is, however, one more moment to suggest that it holds some relevance.

In the Sixties, early on in our relationship, in fact so early that Diana was still prepared to drive me to fishing and either wait for me, listening to *Round the Horn,* or return for me later, we were held up at a small level crossing, the water glinting beyond the gates. Sitting there, without complaining but tense and frustrated, I became the object of speculation and hardly to my credit.

'If we were in London,' said Diana after a long pause, 'I'd suppose you were dreaming about girls, but as we're here I suppose it's those fucking trout!'

Those 'girls' are now middle-aged ladies, but the 'fucking trout', or at any rate their descendants, still face upstream beyond, if it still exists, that level crossing, of course elsewhere.

I suggested a little earlier I write only for other fishermen. This is not exactly a lie, but the whole truth, like most angling authors, except perhaps for those who write textbooks and maybe even them, is that I am writing mostly for myself. I know too that my place is amongst that ninety per cent of the anglers who catch only ten per cent of the fish and have resigned myself to remaining in that majority until my death. My object here, pratfalls and all, is to repay a lifetime's debt to hours of frustrating pleasure and pleasurable frustration. My hope is that I don't become too gaga or arthritic to wait for the evening rise.

If I could choose a death, even beyond collapsing in the wings of a theatre after a sell-out concert, the applause the last sound I'd hear, it would be to be discovered on a river bank dead but with a smile on my face, and a big, beautifully marked trout on the grass beside me.

PART 1

CHILDHOOD

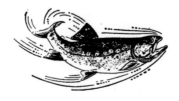

1

'WELL DONE, YOUNG FELLER'

Does a river run through the womb? Is a love of fishing genetic? I suspect not. It's true that my father and grandfather fished and I loved and admired them both, but my father was equally keen on golf and shooting, neither of which attracted me at all.

Nor for my part have I been able to interest my son Tom, although in his case his green sensibility may have put him off. Some years ago he wandered down to watch me fishing on the Welsh Usk and almost immediately I was into a trout. In front of him I played it, netted it, and then killed it with two bangs on the head and three more to be certain; this dispatch five seconds in all. As I rose to my feet and began to cast again, Tom observed, although not aggressively, that it was a pity that so elegant an activity should end by extinguishing a life. It didn't stop him eating it later, though. He, like many who find fishing cruel but believe that a fish on a plate is perfectly acceptable, remind me of Lewis Carroll's Walrus and his requiem for the oysters.

> 'I weep for you,' the Walrus said,
> 'I deeply sympathise.'
> With sobs and tears he sorted out those of the largest size,
> Holding his pocket handkerchief before his streaming eyes.
>
> *Through the Looking-Glass*, Lewis Carroll

Later I shall be obliged to try to answer the charge of cruelty, ranging as it does from mild liberal worry to the spoiling tactics of the Fish-sabs. Nor would I deny that in fishing there is an element of cruelty involved, but I would also say this: I have never watched an angler deliberately play a fish longer than was necessary to grass it, or, with one exception, seen a fisherman express, whether through word or body language, the least indication of sadistic pleasure at killing his quarry.

And the exception? It was an old film-clip, part of a TV documentary. It showed a short, military figure marching up and down in front of a row of large salmon, presumably caught by him and hanging by the tail from a multiple scaffold. They were all obviously dead, but every now and then he'd whack one of them viciously on the skull with a priest. For those tempted to imagine some Buñuel-like image at this point, 'a priest' is the name given by tackle shops to a small wooden club capped with a brass helmet. In this particular case the name was quite appropriate as a symbol of the support the clergy had given the fish-basher during the Civil War. It was General Franco. Perhaps he was imagining the salmon were Basque Anarchists.

15 August 1935, two days before my ninth birthday, next to my father in the back of my grandfather's Armstrong Siddeley. My grandfather always sat next to his chauffeur because as an ex-colonel, albeit of a territorial regiment, he liked to think of him as his batman.

I was in a state of high, if suppressed, excitement. For the first time, after much pleading and sulking, I had persuaded them to take me 'grown-up' fishing, that is to say fishing for trout, their previous reluctance based on the perfectly possible supposition that I might get rapidly bored, demanding and a pest.

My moustached grandfather, whistling through his rather ill-fitting false teeth as usual, would have been dressed in a three-piece tweed suit, a butterfly collar, and a grey homburg hat. My father, nurtured by the Twenties, would have been more in the casual style of the Prince of Wales. The chauffeur wore a maroon uniform with matching cap and polished black gaiters.

I had already done some fishing before, but didn't think of it as 'proper' fishing. At Coniston, in the Lake District, we sometimes spent our holidays in a pretty Regency house belonging to an elderly relative. There, on calm days and accompanied by an

11

adult, we were allowed out in a dinghy to live-bait (with wretched minnows) for rather disappointingly small perch. We never tried to eat them, although they are said to be rather good, if bony, but killed them nevertheless and fed them to the near-feral cats on the home farm.

Once there was a moment of excitement. My float went under, but when I reeled in, instead of a feeble spined perch there was an indolent, green and yellow, four-pound pike on the line. Not for long, though. It took us in with cold blasé contempt, and sank into the depths again, snapping the cast without any effort at all.

I had done some mackerel fishing too, in a pitching boat off Trearddur Bay, Angelsea, but the streamline blue and silver fish were so eager, once you'd located them, to impale themselves on the large, crudely feathered hooks that it soon became monotonous.

No, *real* fishing, or so I'd gathered by listening to my father, my grandfather, and various male cousins and uncles, was the pursuit of trout or salmon using an artificial fly. To this end my father would sometimes stay in fishing hotels, but most often he would take advantage of the generosity of his Uncle Willy. He was in fact the *deus ex machina*, the generator of those circumstances which accounted for three generations sitting in a motor car juddering down a dusty, pot-holed lane in North Wales en route to the River Clwyd that hot August afternoon.

From the Twenties on, Uncle Willie, considered too frail to

be more than a part-time businessman, was nevertheless passionate about shooting and fishing and, being rich through the exertions of his father and grandfather, hired sporting estates every summer, to which the whole extended family were welcome to take advantage, although my father's generation was expected to rent a cottage or farmhouse in the neighbourhood if they intended to remain there for any length of time. Otherwise we had *carte blanche*, eating as often as we wished the huge Edwardian meals, playing tennis or croquet, and of course shooting or fishing if these were of interest to us.

For our comfort and entertainment silver, glass, linen, wine and servants were all transplanted from Liverpool, while as hostess there was Uncle Willy's elderly and rather formidable sister Eva, who had a face like a cross pug-dog and dressed like Queen Victoria.

By the time I was old enough to be fully aware of this annual migration poor Uncle Willy, never robust in health, had suffered some kind of comparatively mild stroke. Until then he had, I understand, been prepared to shoot and fish all day and stay up until the small hours playing cards and talking. My father described him, pre-stroke, as 'boisterous' (a word like 'dressy', never indicating his full approval). Post-stroke he became, on the contrary, completely lethargic, saying very little, smoking constantly through an ivory and amber holder, drinking brandy and soda all day long in an armchair in front of a lit fire, for he was always cold whether in winter or summer, Wales or Liverpool.

Yet though unable to shoot or fish himself, and seemingly indifferent to his surroundings, he unselfishly continued to hire estates and went on doing so until 1937. In the winter of that year his sister Eva died, and a fortnight later my grandfather, only in his sixties, of an undetected ulcer. The following summer Uncle Willy stayed on at Chatham Street and, so far as I know, never left it again until his own death during, but not as a result of, the blitz.

*   *   *   *   *

Half-way down the lane we stopped to allow a mallard and her large brood to cross in front of us. People, and I have done it myself, tend to describe those moments, especially when connected with childhood and of no obvious significance in themselves, but which nevertheless flash across the inner eye for no apparent reason, as 'snapshots'. I now think of them, in that they tend to move, more like a few frames of film. In my memory those ducks still cross that lane, dappled by the sunlight of sixty years ago.

Of course it was a charming and touching sight and all of us, especially my grandfather who adored the more sentimental anthropomorphic aspect of Walter Disney's early 'Silly Symphonies', made suitable gruff noises; but although I too saw the charm of this maternal spectacle, my principal feeling was of irritation. 'Jemima' and her pretty family were holdinig us up!

*   *   *   *   *

At last, though, we were at the river and there was a fishing hut smelling of creosote, and outside my father and grandfather put up their beautiful split-cane rods, attached their reels, threaded their lines through the eyeholes and tied on the cat-gut casts (called leaders now) which, unlike post-war nylon, had to be soaked overnight in a wash-basin to straighten out the kinks. I watched all this with close attention; later I must learn to do it, to tie those complicated knots that father and son managed with such dexterity. Then out came their trout-fly boxes, but there was very little hesitation. Of course they were wet-fly fishing and it is probably less essential that the artificial insect which the trout takes under water as seemingly drowned or drowning and carried round on the current, should be as accurate as a dry fly, floating down over the trout on the surface, and as close an imitation as possible to the hatch among which it bobs, or at any rate of a seasonally appropriate nature: each month has its own flies both terrestrial and aquatic.

Indeed my father had a very sketchy knowledge of flies – 'any drab little thing' was his all-purpose ruling – and I too tended to follow his advice, but I regret it, now that I am almost exclusively dry-fly fishing. I feel forced to try to learn more.

At last they were ready (how elegant and minimal are the engines of fly-fishing, especially in those split-cane days) and turned their attention to my needs. I knew of course that I wouldn't be fly-fishing – later on, if I was still keen, my father had promised to teach me to cast, but for the moment I would worm. Even so he put me up a proper, if fairly small, rod, a child's rod in fact, yet perfect in every detail. This, like the child's dinner-jacket hanging, well mothballed, in a wardrobe in distant Chatham Street, went back several generations and my grandfather and possibly his father had learnt the basics on it. On the end of the cast my father tied a hook; actually a stripped, past-it old salmon-fly, for there was little coarse-fishing equipment in the rod-room. They had, however, and rather surprisingly, found a float there, and slid this up to where the rather short cast met the line, and added several lead pellets to stop the whole thing floating downstream on the current. I watched all this with mounting excitement and just suppressed impatience; my father always took anything and every-thing slowly. I wish I had inherited this approach to both life and fishing.

Finally he pulled out of his pocket an old tobacco tin, the lid punctured with holes. He had filled it with damp moss and, in the moss, was a writhing mass of large earthworms he had dug up that morning in the kitchen garden. He chose one and threaded it, wriggling vigorously, on the hook but leaving, as he pointed out to me, some tail free to twitch and dangle. Then he found a small backwater in the bank, protected from the pull of the current but obviously quite deep, and here we dropped in the bait and I sat down, warmed by the August sun, to watch the float which he advised me not to keep pulling impatiently out of the water to look at.

And so he strolled upriver to join his father, wondering no

doubt how long it would be before I came wandering and whining along to complain of terminal boredom.

But I was not bored, not for a moment. I watched the float bobbing a little. I could see the chauffeur leaning against the fishing hut reading a paper, and my father fishing a hundred yards away, with my grandfather sitting on a shooting-stick smoking one of his Turkish cigarettes and no doubt remonstrating with my father (which, as I discovered later, was habitual when they fished together) for 'flogging the water'. 'Wait', he'd tell him, 'until there's a trout or two moving. If they're not taking real flies why should they look at yours?'

He was probably right (although sometimes on an apparently dead river a trout will rise), and I have tried to follow his advice even if, after a certain time, my father's impatience tends to break through. Now and then I would pull the worm up to the surface and, finding it still there and wriggling, let it sink again into the mysterious depths.

Then there was nature, which I have always loved and which on a riverbank tends to be especially rewarding and various: a moving riverscape within a still landscape, while the angler's comparative progress, even if casting over several pools, is slow enough to allow the eye to digest, of necessity, much more than those who walk for exercise alone.

We are obliged to be aware of the traffic of insects in the grasses, the geometrical choreography of swifts or swallows feeding on a hatch of fly, a statue-like heron clattering up when alarmed, like a latter-day archaeopterix, the slow passage of clouds, the Impressionist effect of the distant landscape, the pre-Raphaelite detail of the riverbank, the water-birds galore, from imperious swan to cheeky wagtail, the water-rat, vole, fieldmouse, snake, toad, frog, fox, the now-recovering otter, that escapee criminal – the mink, owls and bats at dusk and, of course, the star turn, that smelly little neon-lit glory, the kingfisher, flashing along the opposite bank.

But, and it's an essential but, nature is still, I believe, only an admittedly marvellous bonus for the fisherman, rather than his *raison d'être.* Sometimes, driven mad by the 'I wouldn't have the patience' brigade, we may lie, using nature as the reason we fish, our object to discredit them as insensitive oafs, but in reality how many of us would spend hour after hour on a mile or so of bank without a rod in our hand?

*   *   *   *   *

My father had warned me, just before he'd left to join my grandfather, to shout if anything took and he would come at once. This was because it would probably be an eel and they were tricky, slimy, self-knotting creatures to deal with on the bank. I must have been sitting there for at least an hour when my float bobbed for the first time. Then it did it twice again, but I knew from Coniston not to strike before it went right under. This it did, and everything went mad. Instead of the feeble twitches of a small perch, the line screamed off the reel and I became aware for the first time of that taut, constantly shifting angle between moving line and the surface of the water. The rod was bent almost double and I'd no idea what to do.

My father came running, followed at a more leisurely trot by my grandfather with the net, but when Tom saw how the rod was behaving he knew it was no eel, however big. It might even be, he told his father, a small salmon.

I stood up to fight and my father stood behind me telling me how to manage – when to let the line run, when to reel it in, when to hold it. We hadn't seen it up until then, when suddenly it leapt high out of the water. 'Honour it with your rod,' shouted my father, grasping my wrists and forcing the rod tip down until the great speckled wonder, in its shower of liquid diamonds, rejoined its natural element (in the air the cast is more likely to part). Finally it rose to the surface and began to turn over on its side, the sign of abdication. Twice my grandfather got the net under it, twice it ran again, but finally he was successful, swung the net up and the fish, framed in mesh, was on the bank. Within seconds, priest in hand, my father transformed it into a wonderful still life. Later, back at the fishing hut, we weighed it – three pounds. It was entered in the fishing book:

Date	River	Fish	Fly	Weight	Remarks
August 15th, 1935	*Clwyd*	*Brown trout*	*Worm*	*3 lbs*	*GM's first trout*

19

I sat, for a further two hours, watching the float (my father had threaded a new worm on the hook). Gradually nature reasserted her tranquil and compensatory, dragonfly-punctuated presence; during my battle a thousand kingfishers could have flashed past in close formation and I wouldn't have noticed them. Now I relived that extraordinary twenty minutes, knew it was unlikely to happen again, but then. . .

The great fish lay on the bank beside me. My father, always very sensitive to my needs, had left it there. For me it was an object of love and pride. Suddenly it occurs to me for the first time that that long communion with my first trout during my 'latent period' may have accounted, thirty years or so later, for my solitary act of piscatorial onanism on that long, almost impenetrable island the other end of Wales.

At last, my father having 'flogged the water' fruitlessly, my grandfather almost out of Turkish cigarettes, we drove back to the rented manor to show my trout to everybody above and below stairs. Even Uncle Willy was quite impressed. 'Well done young feller,' he said and handed me half-a-crown.

*   *   *   *   *

I went fishing on the Clwyd several more times that summer holidays, but, although I didn't hook anything else, not even an eel, was in no way put off. During the winter my father taught me how to cast a fly, and I became comparatively proficient, at least on the lawn in Liverpool. I learnt from him, however, a bad, or at any rate academically bad, habit that I have still not overcome: the use of my wrist to shoot the fly out over the water instead of a stiff lower arm. In later years I was reprimanded for this by experts both amateur and professional who, while admitting I can cast quite a long and fairly straight line, begged or ordered me to correct this tendency, if necessary by tucking the reel end of the rod into my sleeve so as to hold the wrist rigid, but I never saw it really mattered. Certainly my father used his wrist and taught me to do so. Presumably his father, who taught him, did the same. Neither had ever considered going to an expert, if indeed they then existed. Perhaps they picked up a certain amount from gillies but probably offered as tentative suggestion rather than holy writ. It's not that I don't wish I'd had lessons, indeed I still could, but, at seventy-four, would feel a little embarrassed among the pink and white youngsters a-buzz with mobile phones.

*   *   *   *   *

The following year on the Clwyd I fished often but caught nothing. I never got desperate, though, never even considered giving up. This may sound smug, but it isn't. It means simply that built into my nature, into the nature of all anglers, and no more to do with virtue than the shape of one's nose, is the one element without which you will never be drawn towards the river bank. It's not, as I've already stressed, 'patience', and of course I didn't recognise or define it for many years. It is *anticipation*.

It is anticipation that, however fishless our endeavours, keeps alive the belief that the next cast, the next hour, the next day, month or season, the trout will take, the rod bend. Inherited? I don't know, but inherent? Yes, certainly.

* * * * *

There was, however, one tremendous excitement for that otherwise empty summer of 1936. It had rained heavily late in August and the river level had risen. Now it was set fair and the water was going down again and clearing fast and Tom thought some salmon might be up although the Clwyd was not a famous salmon river like its neighbour the Welsh Dee.

With this possibility in view he put up a heavy rod, single-handed, not double, but heavy nevertheless (he let me hold it for a moment and I could hardly lift it, let alone cast it). Then he attached a big reel, a strong line and a thick leader. Finally he tied on a gaudy fly – the age of the drab tube was almost twenty years into the future – and began to cast. After not too long, my chore was to bear the large long-handled net, I saw the line unwinding steadily off the reel and off up the pool. Thinking he hadn't noticed I drew it to his attention. He nodded but did nothing for a few more moments before raising the rod. The salmon came to furious life. It ran, jumped, sulked on the bottom and tried all those strategies not once but many times, and Tom ran in its wake up and down the bank while I trailed self-importantly behind with the net and, all the while my father pleaded with the fish like a discarded lover begging his mistress not to leave him, 'Please stay hooked, please oh please! Don't get off! Please don't get off, oh please!'

And at last, it seemed like hours but was probably at most twenty minutes, it began to tire and he gave me the rod to hold while he netted it, both hands necessary to swing it ashore. It was a silver, fresh-run cock-fish with the sea-lice still on it and about ten pounds in weight. It had swum across the great oceans to the very river where it was hatched, avoiding many dangers: seal, killer whale, and the nets at the estuary, driven by the biological imperative to reach the head waters and fertilise the eggs in the troughs called redds, the eggs concealed under gravel spread with a sweeping tail. There the salmon's destiny was fulfilled. Reduced to a hideous near-skeleton, with huge jaws, it would have drifted back to the sea, a kelt, and there it might have 'mended', although the chances were against it. But this particular salmon would never lose its milt in the gravel beds. It had fallen victim to a Liverpool woolbroker.

For those appalled by this intervention, a few disclaimers. Over the years and increasingly, various fishing societies have brought out the nets, declared a controlled policy of catch and return. In many cases they have built ladders to help the fish up difficult stretches of the river, and so on. But the main thing is that these are true salmon and, until caught, fulfil their life-cycle. Most supermarkets and restaurant salmon these days are caged in the sea lochs and fed chemicals to encourage their rapid growth. They taste of nothing and spread diseases amongst wild migratory fishing passing through. As with battery chickens interested parties put forward the argument that salmon, once the preserve of the well-to-do, is now cheap and available to all, but like battery chickens they are without flavour, often dyed a fake pink, and a shadow of the real thing, pathetic victims of commercial exploitation.

Not that my father could have foreseen any of this. It's true that trout farms already existed, but if well run, and trout being non-migratory, there is no comparison with the imprisonment of its cousin with its complicated and far-ranging genetic impulses, its long migration and hazardous return.

*　*　*　*　*

Rereading what I've written to date, I will now make a promise. But for exceptional circumstances, I will no longer describe in any detail the hooking and landing of a fish. No more 'tight lines' or 'screaming reels' – take them as read.

*　*　*　*　*

In 1936, while still unable to get out a long line, my casting, practised initially on the lawn in Liverpool, had much improved, but that August I caught nothing, although a rare 'knock' on the line was enough, if not essential, to keep my anticipation alive.

In 1937 Uncle Willy rented yet again the yellow pebble-dashed manor house with its rods on the River Clwyd. In earlier years we had B and B'd in farmhouses, but this time (was the wool business improving?) Tom had rented a fairly small white house in the 'modernistic' style on the outskirts of Denbigh and had even bought, for ten pounds, an old car, built in the Twenties, for those rare occasions when my grandfather's Armstrong Siddeley wasn't available. He used it especially to cross the border on Sunday mornings. The pre-lunch drink in a pub was sacred to him, and in Wales in those days and for a long time afterwards there was no drinking on the begloved, prayer-book-grasping Sabbath and, come to that, no fishing either. The car, which looked as if it must break down any minute and which Tom called 'the Heap', proved an excellent investment. It went back and forth to Liverpool when business insisted he return, carried us into Rhyl or Prestatyn most mornings to swim in the great public art deco swimming pools, and of course, we took it down to the river. That year my grandfather came with us less often. He had become rather lethargic, the effect perhaps of the ulcer which was to kill him the following winter.

My father and I didn't do at all well – August is notoriously a bad month for trout. He hooked only two (he unselfishly let me land one of them). But he had hatched a little plot.

At the end of the quite long garden behind the 'Bauhaus to Our House' villa ran a small stream about twenty yards long and, at its widest point, five yards across. Convinced, with the if-wishes-were-horses optimism of the child (childish tyro?) that there were trout in it, and in no way put off by the times I became entangled in trees on the opposite bank (it was shallow enough to wade across and release or, if too high up, break off the fly), I 'flogged the water' hour after hour.

My father, who knew perfectly well it was troutless, put forward the theory that there were too many leaves and other rubbish floating down it, and to 'cure' this bought some posts with pointed ends and small-meshed wire-netting and we built a barrier at each end – I have a film clip of him doing this with his trousers rolled up – taking especial care that there were no gaps along the bottom.

That evening after dinner when I was asleep he drove 'the Heap' to the nearest trout farm with a bucket by his side and returned with six quarter-pound trout in it, which he released into the stream where, eventually, I hooked one.

My mother was summoned with the Box Brownie and snapped me, rod in one hand, small fish in the other, and wearing an absurdly proud expression. It was very blurred yet perfectly readable.

*   *   *   *   *

I failed to land any of the other five, perhaps they had discovered a gap under the barriers despite my father's care. Naturally I didn't even know there were five left then. It wasn't until several years later than he told me how he had deceived me. Far from upset, I was rather moved by his imaginative strategy.

*　*　*　*　*

No fishing the next year; my grandfather and his older sister in their grave. None before the war, none during and none almost ten years after it. Was I desperate? Did I miss it? Strangely enough, no. I seemed cured – detoxed.

2

A TWITCH
UPON THE
LINE

I have often wondered why, after such an encouraging apprenticeship, I didn't put up a rod again for over fifteen years, but when I did I found out that my addiction wasn't cured but had only been latent, lulled by circumstances, banished by more pressing needs and sensations.

First came the war, evacuation, the blitz and my father's involvement, first as an ARP warden on the Liverpool docks, later as a lieutenant in the 'wavy navy'. Then I was sent to Stowe School, Bucks, where I discovered Surrealism, jazz, W. H. Auden and how to avoid, when possible, compulsory games. There was acting, too, both school and house plays, and a series of romantic or purely lecherous 'affairs' with my contemporaries, consummated in dormitory, study, the art school puppet theatre or the well-wooded and by now mature grounds laid out by Capability Brown at the command of that periwigged Duke of Buckingham to show off his wonderful great house.

Yet among the temples, follies and obelisks were a series of artificial lakes containing coarse fish and I heard that some boys made use of them. I myself was untempted. Snobbery came into it, certainly. Even my father, the least snobbish of men, and certainly my grandfather, held the view that only trout and salmon were proper fish, besides, to quote Dorothy Parker, I was too fucking busy, or vice versa, untempted by the great carp rooting under the lily pads.

Joining the Royal Navy in 1944 made no difference. Training in North Wales in an ex-Butlins holiday camp (surely there was trout fishing available within reach) I re-met by chance a schoolfriend and fellow Surrealist-enthusiast who had discovered, in the advertising columns of *The New Statesman*, that it was possible to order publications from the Surrealist Group in London and this we did and, at the same time, sent them some of my friend's Ernst-like collages and my own derivative poems. We received a friendly answer and later, stationed for a year on an overflow ship in Chatham Dockyard (they'd lost me) I got in touch, joined the movement, and became an intimate friend of its leader, E. L. T. Mesens and his wife Sybil.

Eventually I was discovered at Chatham, and posted to a real ship, HMS *Dido*, on which I was to spend the remaining year-and-a-half of my life as an able seaman. The war was by now over and I thoroughly enjoyed the 'goodwill' tours abroad. I felt no enthusiasm, however, when, during my last few months in bell bottoms, we were ordered to join other ships of the line in a bleak sea loch enclosed by small islands to the north of Scotland. We were there to 'paint ship' ready for a royal review of the Fleet in the Clyde some ten days hence. Unless, as a bawdy member of my messdeck pointed out, you were a sheep-shagger, there was no point in going ashore, or at least not for the crew, but early one morning, when I was on watch on the quarterdeck, two officers, the first lieutenant and the ship's doctor in tweeds and burberries were rowed ashore armed with nets and fishing-rods and, for the first time in years, a certain hunger stirred in me.

*   *   *   *

This was confirmed and heightened later. Being at anchor I was on duty at the gang-plank as temporary quartermaster, a job I held only when in harbour, for at sea I would have been expected to take the wheel, and no one would have trusted me in that role.

In the small hours, the Middle Watch, as I believe it was called, I was on duty again, sharing the four hours with a corporal of the Marines. Despite the company it was very boring because absolutely nothing happened. We filled in the time with mutual masturbation (the corporal, who was, I'm sure, almost completely heterosexual, to give him something to do, whereas I, who was still ninety per cent gay, because he was a handsome lad). When this was over, we raided the galley of the officers' mess, a rather exciting and dangerous adventure involving, as it did, deserting our post. We were after eggs, never more than two, and bacon, if there were sufficient rashers to pass unnoticed, which we cooked, rather dangerously, in a small frying pan on an electric fire turned on its back in our little caboosh (cabin) where the incident book was kept. Sometimes too there was a half-eaten bowl of pudding, cheese and other delicacies.

On this occasion there was something else, something which excited me far more than any liberated titbits. On a large white oval dish lay the successful outcome of the two officers' expedition. The ship's doctor and first lieutenant between them had returned onboard earlier with five or six beautiful brown trout of about a pound and a half each, and there they were.

My atavistic instincts, together with a certain impotent, egalitarian rage that only officers had been entitled to cast for them, flooded my whole being. I stared at them for so long that the corporal had to grab my arm to remind me of the risk we were running.

I knew then that I would fish again, but where and when was an open question. I ate my bacon and eggs in a near trance, dreaming of running water, skies at dusk and the widening rings

of rising fish. The corporal, unaccustomed to my silence, asked if
I'd had bad news from home.

*   *   *   *   *

There were still several years to go before I realised my renewed
ambition. Demobbed a few months later, I returned to Liverpool
for six weeks to attempt and fail to learn shorthand typing and
then moved permanently to work at E. L. T. Mesens's reopened
London Gallery. An unhappy two years followed, as I was a
hopeless and innumerate employee (E. L. T., Surrealist by night,
was a martinet by day), but I very soon discovered the British
revivalist jazz world and began to sing with various more or less
obscure bands. I eventually joined Mick Mulligan and we soon
achieved a certain *succès de scandale*. When the gallery closed in
1950 (Surrealism was completely out of fashion after the war),
Mick proposed we turned professional, and we stayed on the road,
not earning much, but having a wild alcoholic and libidinous time,
laced with squalor, for the next twelve years. During this time we
were booked for many three-week tours of Scotland and for a
comparatively long period. Our bass player was a complex and
interesting man called Gerry Salisbury.

Gerry, because he moved as if wearing a neck-brace and
spoke only after considerable thought, gave the impression that he
might be a little slow-witted, but he was nothing of the kind. A
good bass player, he was also a fine and original trumpet player,

but after a few numbers his lip packed in. He also had an interesting history. His family were Cockney working-class and had lived for many generations in Covent Garden. Their life, as he described it to me in his episodic way, was rather Dickensian: there was a long-standing feud with a local copper and so on, but Gerry had married into the northern suburbs, a step up, I suppose, but I got the impression that, although he was far too loyal to admit it, he may have regretted it. In the context of this book, however, what matters is that he was an enthusiastic angler.

Coarse fish only, however. I asked him if he had ever tried fly-fishing and he replied quite definitively in the negative. His reason was based on his proud but un-chippy working-class conservatism. Fly-fishing, he explained, was for gentlemen. He was working-class. Coarse fishing was working man's sport. There was no point in arguing. It struck me that it was the mirror image of what my father and grandfather believed, and actually a late Victorian and especially an Edwardian concept. Izaak Walton treated all fish with equal respect and usually gave recipes for almost all of them, even the most muddy and tasteless. Jerry of course killed none, with the exception (although he had by that time never caught one) of the pike. The rest he kept prisoner in a keep-net, counting and weighing them at the end of the day and then releasing them.

In the past few decades Gerry's dictum has lost most of its *raison d'être*. The proliferation of trout farms, the majority of them adjacent to lakes, reservoirs or large ponds, has led to their owners stocking these still waters with largely rainbow trout, some of great size, where, for day or season ticket, anglers can fly-fish for a comparatively reasonable sum. The equipment is, it's true, even then rather expensive, but you need very little: rod, reel, line and a few spools of the new nylon leader of various strength, a handful of artificial flies. Coarse fishermen, on the contrary, accumulate an enormous amount of tackle: numerous rods and reels, huge poles with additional extensions like a snooker cue, floats, variegated hooks, line and leger-weights, tiered and hinged boxes, a maggot tin or apron, the expanding keep-net itself – the list is formidable. What's more, new developments and refinements appear con-stantly in the shops or the advertising columns of the coarse fishing journals or newspapers and are a constant temptation. No plumber or carpenter is better or more heavily equipped than a coarse angler setting out for a day by the water.

Nor, today, does Gerry's class barrier hold up. You may, of course, pay a fortune to fish on the hallowed chalk streams of Hampshire, but it isn't necessary. Most trout farms, of which there are a proliferation, in keeping with the proliferating supermarkets stocked with pallid, identically sized rainbows, who, if adjacent to a lake, reservoir, pool or even sizeable pond, release some of their stock for the benefit of anglers. These ventures vary enormously in management and quality, but except for a handful, which are almost as expensive as the chalk streams, they charge a reason-able amount by the season, day or half-day, and a fair number of 'working men' have transferred their allegiance.

Many haven't, though. Our drummer, Eddie Taylor, a Lancastrian by birth and a fanatical and encyclopaedic coarse fisherman by temperament, gave still-water fly-fishing a try and, perfectionist as he is, became successful at it, pleased also to take the permitted number of fish home to eat them. I thought he'd be won over, but not at all. He has reverted largely to the keep-net and the maggot.

This widespread facility means also that those counties, Kent, Essex, the Midlands and Norfolk, which, in most cases, famous for coarse fish but lacking, due to being very flat, those fast-running rivers or streams necessary to hatch wild trout, have stocked still waters within easy driving distance and of course most anglers now have cars. For those, and not always old, who turn up their noses, it is a dirty little secret, an open reference to which is the equivalent of the Victorian taboo of mentioning a lady's name in the mess, that these days, of necessity, even the poshest chalk streams are partially stocked, admittedly with local brown trout released in the autumn so they have to become used to earning their own living over the winter, and thus become as good as wild, or nearly so, by the opening of the season, but they are stocked fish nevertheless. My grandfather must be turning in his grave, but then he of course was born into the high noon of side-whiskered purism.

As for myself, I will admit to preferring running water, and brown trout to the alien rainbow, but when, either from lack of oppportunity, or those long stretches when no river trout has even a look at my fly, or else overcome by the addict's need to fish out of season (for on still water there is no need to honour the breeding months and many are open the whole year except usually on Christmas Day), I don't hesitate to spend the day casting on the nearest lake, pond or reservoir and usually with satisfactory, and occasionally sensational, results.

*   *   *   *   *

Gerry's personal credo didn't stop him accompanying me on my first, rather nervous, return to a river in almost fifteen years. We were somewhere in the Scottish borders, fulfilling a series of gigs for a lovable if whisky-sodden promoter called 'Drunken Duncan' (not that this failing diminished him in the bloodshot eyes of the Mick Mulligan band, all of whom, with the exception of Pete Appleby, a South London mythomaniac, whose total abstention usually meant he won heavily at poker, were committed to what our leader called 'a noggin').

I put up my rod by the side of a modest stream. I'd remembered most of it, although initially I had the reel facing to the left whereas (there is no fixed rule) I prefer the handle to the right. What I'd totally forgotten, however, were the knots needed to tie the cast (now leader) to the line at one end and the fly at the other. Naturally these knots need to be as small and light as you can make them and mine were like a piece of wool after the attention of a hyper-active kitten. Luckily Gerry came to the rescue.

My first cast was clumsy, but I improved a little during the afternoon, despite hooking several tries and creating several birds' nests (again, he unravelled these in no time at all). And then, quite unexpectedly, a trout rose and remained hooked. I landed it; there was no need to use my brand-new net either, it was so small that it made the near-minnows of my father's stocking of the stream at 'Lount' seem like Leviathans. It was beautifully marked, however, and put up a minuscule fight, or at least didn't give itself up spontaneously. First wetting my hands – I remembered you should always do this, as dry skin can activate a fungus (Is this true, by the way? I still do it, of course, but have sometimes wondered) I then removed the fly as gently as I could and tossed the fingerling back into the water. Here I was grievously at fault. It was some time before someone told me, rather censoriously, that you should hold a trout of whatever size under the surface and facing upstream for some moments to let it get over the shock, and only then let it go and watch it, usually after a pause, as though it couldn't believe its luck, dart off to resume its hazardous life among its natural predators, scaled or feathered.

Gerry, I suspect, was rather impressed that I released it. Perhaps he thought that 'gentlemen' killed everything, whatever the size. For the rest of the afternoon nothing happened, but, as we were returning to the hotel and its vast high tea, he remarked, with the kindness that was part of his nature, that at least I'd proved I hadn't forgotten how to do it, and that was true. That 'wee fush' was the equivalent of the sherry in the trifle that triggers

37

off the long-time abstemious alcoholic. There was to be no more remission. I was hooked again, and this time for keeps.

*   *   *   *   *

And so, for the final stretch of the Mulligan band's existence I continued to fish on our frequent summer tours of the Scottish Borders and points north. In general I didn't often score, although now and again, and still to my surprise, I would land the odd fish, but most often, almost inevitably, returned empty-handed.

The Mulligan band were not known for their courteous behaviour to one another. Needling was general, and in particular Ian Christie, whose savage impaling of the failings of his colleagues earned him the nickname 'the Shrike', after an insect-eating bird which stores its victims on thorns until next feeling peckish, was perhaps favourite, but Mick too was an expert at deflating any signs of pretension or bullshit. Nor was I noted for my tolerance or willingness to let ignorance or cant slip by. It was a hard school and any new replacements took some time to accept it.

Frank Parr, trombonist, fellow-Liverpudlian, ex-wicket keeper for Lancashire and intransigent enthusiast for the gamy aroma of his own armpits, had his own method of putting the boot in. He would note any effective put-down of a colleague's behaviour, and then if, as was so often the case, the alleged failing proved permanent, he would quietly but inevitably repeat the verbal quip that it had originally provoked, but in the form of a question. This was not only irritating but also satisfied Frank's almost Catholic fondness for ritual. An example, cited by me years ago in my first book, but a very clear demonstration: we had a bass player at one time who, although enviably thin, frequently consumed a bar of chocolate on long journeys in the band wagon. He would try to do this as discreetly as possible, but it never escaped Frank. When somebody first noted this addiction, whoever it was speculated aloud as to the possibility of a tapeworm being responsible. Someone else quoted a very obscene limerick, known to us all, of which the last line reads 'If Jimmy, the tape-worm, don't seize yer'. In conclusion, therefore, we decided it was 'Jimmy' who demanded the endless bars of Dairy Milk. It quite annoyed the bass player, who had not long joined us and was anyway inclined to stand on his dignity, but, in general, it would probably have been consigned to the cellar of past teases or only occasionally recalled, *but not with Frank around*. Every time the chocolate bar appeared, but *every* time, Frank would politely pose this question, 'Jimmy time, Alan?' and every time, although he had the good sense not to show it, you could tell it irritated Alan beyond measure.

When it came to my fishing expeditions, however, Frank had no need to resurrect an earlier flick of the verbal whip. I have little doubt that, for Frank, fishing for trout formed an item on his personal and extensive list which went under the general heading of 'Pretentious Bollocks', but in my case he didn't resort to an open attack. His ploy here, following my return and noting the absence of any of the angler's inevitable suppressed indication of triumph, was to wait until some, or if possible all, the band were present, and then ask me with apparently mild interest if I'd caught anything. Night after night of this, although naturally I took care never to show any reaction beyond a neutral answer in the negative, had, as was intended, the dispiriting effect of the Chinese water torture.

I was, however, to have my revenge on Francis Parr.

*   *   *   *   *

One fine afternoon, Ian Christie, the new recruit, and myself were fishing a rather larger stream than usual. It was fine and sunny now, but there had been some heavy rain, although the water was going down and clearing fast. Ian was about a hundred yards upstream. My pool was quite wide, with a small bay on the opposite bank. Suddenly, well of course suddenly, I was into a fish and after quite a tussle grassed it. It looked like a trout, but silvery and unspeckled. It turned out to be a young sea-trout and weighed just over the pound. I killed it with a heavy stone for I didn't possess a priest – I quite often don't own one now. It is easy, following the excitement of catching a fish, to leave it in the grass, although I'm learning, rather late in the day, to overcome this expensive and careless habit, and anyway a stone of the right size and shape, if rather less elegant, is just as efficient, and I always keep one in my fishing bag.

40

I stood up and cast again and almost immediately hooked another and then another, all of about the same weight, until there were six or seven on the bank. Of course I lost a few, either on the strike or during the fight, but they were in a feeding frenzy, as keen as those stupid mackerel at Trearddur Bay; except of course you couldn't just haul them in. They needed careful playing. I had one on, in the middle of all this excitement, which was much bigger. It went shooting across to the bay and got off; perhaps in my inexperience I was treating it too roughly. The joke at the fisherman's expense relating to 'the one that got away' is most often a truth. The larger fish are heavier, and wiser. They've been hooked before in all probability. Naturally I mildly regretted the loss of this comparative leviathan, but in the midst of such plenty it didn't spoil my excitement. Finally, after about forty minutes, the rise stopped dead. I literally and childishly danced a jig of triumph.

Ian saw me do this and came downstream to see what I was up to. He was impresssed, if naturally a little envious at my success. I, for my part, experienced and still experience, a modicum of guilt. I could easily have afforded, for it was quite a large pool, to have paused for a moment and, attracting his attention, signalled or shouted for him to join me and share my good fortune. Whether through greed or because I was too excited to consider it, I didn't. He, for his part, unshrike-like for once, never reproached me for it. He seemed almost as happy for me as I was.

On the way back to the hotel we plotted how best to turn

the tables on Frank Parr. What we decided on was to sneak in by the kitchen door. There we persuaded the cook-cum-proprietress, for it was a small establishment, to substitute the sea-trout (she knew what they were) for the cold ham or kippers or whatever it was she had planned, and she agreed to do it. It was, after all, a saving on her budget and, stereotype or no stereotype, most Scots are all in favour of that. For an hour Ian and I stayed out of sight, materialising only when the tiny gong in the hall was struck. Frank came in a little late and, before he got round to posing his inevitable question, it was answered in the affirmative by the entrance of the landlady bearing a large and pretty Victorian dish with the sea-trout taking up most of it and beautifully cooked.

The band, of course, previously taking pleasure in Frank's tease, were equally entertained by his discomfiture. They applauded, unjustly, my skill and relished the fish themselves with their firm pink flesh and accompanied by new, parsley-sprinkled potatoes. I can't remember if Frank ate any. It would surely have tasted of soot and ashes if he did. I doubt it anyway. Most food, with the exception of eggs, bacon and chips, well-dowsed with Daddie's Sauce, he defined as 'pretentious bollocks'. From that day on, however, although I was in general no more successful than before, he never asked me if I'd caught anything.

3

DEATH. THE FISHERMAN

Death is a fisherman, the world we see
His fish-pond is and we the fishes be.
He sometimes, angler-like, doth with us play
And slily takes us one by one away.

Anon. *Death's Trade* (17th century)

Once I told my father I'd started fishing again he offered to take me, during the band's holiday, for a short weekend on Lake Vyrnwy in North Wales. My younger brother Bill, recently commissioned in the Royal Navy, although at that time not the keen dry-fly man he was to become in later life, happened to be on leave and he too was asked and accepted.

My mother was pleased that 'the men', as she referred to us collectively, should be going off together, as lately she'd become worried that Tom, while only in his late fifties, had given up his Saturday morning golf. Perhaps my renewed interest in fishing might reanimate him. She waved off 'the men' in high spirits.

My father was at the wheel of his second-hand and slightly rusty Morris. He had finally decided that we did need a car permanently instead of just over the summer holidays, but, while the Morris was decidedly more roadworthy if less picturesque than 'the Heap', it was hardly ostentatious. Cars, like clothes and eating in restaurants, were missing from his list of priorities. No one could have accused him of conspicuous spending.

I was intoxicated with anticipation. We drove through the Mersey Tunnel, through the border town of Wrexham, and up into the Aran Berwyn range of mountains.

The large Victorian hotel crouched like a robber baron's castle high above the long, narrow lake, itself eight hundred feet above sea level.

Having signed the ancient leather-bound visitors' book we found our rooms, Bill and I sharing, Tom on his own. I had been mildly puzzled as to why, while allowing the frail and elderly porter to carry up everything else, my father had insisted on retaining his thigh-waders which he'd slung over his shoulder. All became clear, however, when he invited us into his room advising us to bring our toothbrush glasses with us. Delving down into one of the boots he produced a bottle of Booth's (he preferred it to Gordon's), a smaller bottle of Angostura bitters and mixed us all a stiff pink gin, a drink to which he had become addicted during his wartime stint as 'wavy-navy lieutenant' stationed in Troon, and which Bill was beginning to appreciate in the wardroom.

But why the secrecy? His explanation made perfectly good sense according to his lights. Resenting what he felt to be the exorbitant mark-up in fishing hotels, he chose to undermine it by 'knocking back a few stiff ones' before buying a single in the bar prior to lunch or dinner.

From that day on, whenever I'm on the road with the band and suspect, or know, that our gig will be miles from the nearest pub, which either has no bar, a beer and wine licence only, or closes at the interval, I honour 'the fishing boot' and stop off en route at an off-licence or supermarket, and while tucking the half-bottle of Jameson's into my briefcase, remember with amused affection the three of us drinking warm gin flavoured with bitters and tasting, however faintly, of toothpaste in Tom's hotel bedroom, almost fifty years ago.

That afternoon, armed with the two permitted rods, we drove down to the lake and climbed into the obligatory rowing-boat. In front of us lay 1,121 acres. Originally a river, it was dammed in the 1880s to form a reservoir for thirsty Liverpool. The dam itself is four-and-a-half miles away and invisible from the hotel. The water on calm days, as this was, reflects the dramatic mountainous landscape of North Wales. Lake Vyrnwy, long and narrow as it is, doesn't look man-made at all, and even the one indication that we have had something to do with it is designed to look as if it were long, long ago.

Not far from the hotel's landing stage, just offshore on the right-hand side, is a castellated stone water tower. It exactly subscribes to the convention of the romantic school of painters, to include something on a human scale into a picture, if only in contrast to the awesome grandeur of nature.

Something old though, or seemingly old. The Lake Vyrnwy water-tower looks, if not Arthurian, at any rate Tennysonian, but then I have often noticed how Victorian architects, with few exceptions, seemed to go into Gothic overdrive when commissioned to design anything connected with the commercial exploitation of water, with industry and above all railway stations.

And so, with Bill at the oars, and trolling our two flies behind the boat, we glided out into the middle of the lake, Bill shipped the oars and we began to fish. Tom, going on the evidence of his pre-war visits, was at first convinced the trout would come on at any minute, but they didn't and, not only did they pay us no attention, there were none rising either.

According to a fairly recent guide-book (1984), Lake Vyrnwy is stocked with 2000 rainbows and brown trout per annum and I dare say it was approximately the same in the Fifties. My father, I suspect more on my behalf than his own, became quite cross. In fact I didn't mind much. The Scottish tours had accustomed me to low expectations. We cast on until six p.m. – nothing!

Since that day I've fished many still waters from over-stocked near-puddles to great sheets of water and what I've learnt might have saved the day.

For a start my father was fishing as though on a river. He'd tied on his customary 'drab little thing' and cast, as we all did, only to retrieve it just below the surface. Now if the fish had been rising all might have been well, but they were probably cruising deep down, and the solution, then, is to use a huge fly with googoo eyes and trailing feathers in pastel shades. You let this sink for some considerable time and then pull it back up in a series of short jerks. Hopefully your fly ('lure' is surely a more accurate word for these South American night-club hostesses) may cross the level patrolled by the invisible trout and taken, although what they imagine them to be is a complete mystery. Tom, though, and come to that I, had never heard of the 'Dognobblers' and 'Baby Dolls' of today if he had, he might easily have rejected them on ethical grounds. At the other end of the scale, as a son of the North, he tended to dismiss dry-fly purists and manicured chalk streams as 'sissy'. He had been brainwashed by his father and uncles. It has taken me many years to overcome *his* prejudices.

That evening, before dinner, we stood on the terrace of the hotel, our single bar-paid gins in hand, looking down at the lake far below.

'When I first came here with the Guv'nor,' said Tom (who very occasionally, in evoking his late father, reverted to this usage of Edwardian public schoolboys), 'you could stand here at this time and see trout rising right the way up the whole lake.'

I'm sure he believed this, but it can't have been true or at any rate not without field-glasses. We were far too high up to see even a large trout rising directly below us.

*   *   *   *   *

Next morning, we were to leave after lunch, Tom came into our room to make sure we were awake, to find Bill and me daggers drawn. This was because Bill, via Dartmouth Naval College (albeit transferred during the war to Eaton Hall, home of the Duke of Westminster) where he had a successful innings, followed by his first commission, had naturally developed a certain conventional set of values, whereas I, travelling the roads with Mick Mulligan's Jazz Band, and behaving as badly as we could get away with, shared very little in common. Bill, for example, wore pyjamas, I slept naked, but our bone of contention was to do with relieving our bladders. The lavatory – no *en suite* bathrooms in those days – was at the end of a corridor and Bill, putting on dressing-gown and slippers, made use of it. Our room did, however, contain a wash-basin and, now that there were no cat-guts soaking in it overnight, and me being nude, it seemed to me natural to piss in it, although with, as a concession, the tap running. Bill was very angry, but I paid no notice. When my father came in, Bill complained bitterly. My father, rather to my surprise, took his side, and delivered me a terrible dressing-down. Had his years in the wavy navy had its effect on him too?

'Disgusting!' he thundered. 'Inexcusable! Insanitary!' During this tirade Bill, naturally enough, while forbearing to gloat, looked just a shade smug, as if he'd put me on 'Commander's Defaulters' and proved justified in doing so.

Then, when he'd finished bollocksing me, Tom walked over to the wash-basin and took an enormous leak.

I was, of course, delighted. Bill, naturally enough, less so. In retrospect it was cruel of my father – it was not Bill's fault that he had been brainwashed as a cadet and reflected the code of the wardroom – but it also revealed something in Tom's nature, a largely repressed but deep anarchic streak. His last words to me were, 'Do what you want to. I never did!' Nowadays Bill, I'm sure, would have seen the funny side of it, but not then. He was pretty frosty the whole day.

That morning Tom finally rose a fish. It fought well too, but turned out to be a chub, a handsome creature related to the carp, but despite Izaak Walton, who offers a recipe for everything, entirely uneatable. According to Taverner and Moore, co-authors of the charming *Angler's Week-End Book*, it is 'indistinguishable from a dish composed of a packet of needles, some wet cotton-wool soaked in mud, and a little powdered glass added as a condiment'.

Even so, Tom killed it and placed it – not, I suspect, without a certain irony – on the large china dish provided, with identifying labels to hand, to display guests' baskets in the lobby of the hotel.

*   *   *   *   *

After lunch, Bill still slightly put out, we drove back to Liverpool, but with a slight detour, to visit Tom's older cousin Major Arthur Bromilow, a kindly man personally but of extreme right-wing views, a state no doubt exacerbated as an ex-coalminer owner dislodged by nationalisation. As far as I could tell, from that date on, he was unable to distinguish between Clement Attlee and Joseph Stalin. He lived in a pretty eighteenth-century manor with a cedar on the lawn in front far older than the house itself.

The reason Tom wanted to call was to ask him the best way to join a line to the new nylon cast in that he was nervous that the traditional knot might slip and lose a fish – for Tom, *vide* his anguish with the salmon, the ultimate nightmare – and Cousin Arthur was an acknowledged expert angler. After a delicious dish of crumpets, the old gentleman deftly joined line and leader closely watched by my father, who then thanked him warmly. Back in the car, however, the receding cedar still reflected in the cracked wing mirror, Tom said that in fact Cousin Arthur had shown him the same old knot, but then he was over seventy, getting on a bit. My father was then only fifty-eight.

*   *   *   *   *

The following summer, 1960, Tom booked us into a pub in the Lake District. 'The landlady', he told me, 'sounded very lively on the telephone.' She'd confirmed there was a small trout stream.

It would have been useless to have sued her under the Trades Description Act, if it had existed then, because, after all, the word 'stream' is open to a wide interpretation. In this case it was rather more narrow than the one in Denbigh that Tom had stocked with small trout from the fish-farm. On the other hand, it had wild trout in it, unlikely in those restricted confines to grow much larger, but, as people often say of such Lilliputian fish, 'beautifully marked'.

What's more, that first afternoon, and on the smallest 'drab little thing' in my father's fly-box, I caught one just under a quarter of a pound.

Tom was sitting at a table in front of the pub with a half-pint of draft Bass in front of him, when I ran towards him so that he could share my triumph (at thirty-four I was nothing if not childish), when I stumbled and the tip of his old and beautiful split-cane rod caught a tussock and snapped off. I was desperate, even more so in that I'd been doing exactly what he'd always told me not to: that was to carry a rod facing forward instead of trailing backward, the logic for which had become all too evident, but Tom, rather to my grateful surprise, took it lightly. It could be respliced or replaced. He had a second rod in the car. I was very clever to have caught a fish anyway under so bright a sky, and what would I like to drink?

He had a long rest after lunch while I fished on, this time unsuccessfully. At five minutes to six he came to fetch me. The sun was almost over the yard-arm. Like all dedicated drinkers, myself included, he had several fixed rules; in his case, he never raised a glass between two and six p.m., although on that afternoon, residents in a relaxed country pub, there was nothing to prevent it. He had, however, a mental alarm clock which went off, unheard by anyone but him, five minutes before that sacred moment when landlords, in those days of strict licensing laws, unbolted and unchained their doors and with what, if you were a minute or two early, seemed like deliberate and sadistic slowness, threw open their premises.

I noticed that we went straight into the bar, and the thigh waders, not that they would have been of any practical use in that minuscule stream, stayed in the boot. There were two reasons for this: first, the drinks were at pub prices, though Tom never objected to paying them. Second, however, the landlady, an attractive widow (or divorcee) in her forties, was a skilled flirt of what is now called the laddish persuasion. Tom, while never a Lothario and, I believe, with possibly one exception, to have been faithful to my mother through their whole long marriage, was not averse to flirtation. It probably accounted for his generous offers to pick me up after jazz gigs in Liverpool clubs. The 'mice' (jazz slang for young women fans at that time) flirted with him outrageously, partially at my suggestion.

In any event, our landlady, while by no means a classic

beauty, filled one of my father's criteria – she was 'decorative'.

The dinner, like the lunch, was excellent and served by one of the landlady's beautiful daughters (No, it's not *that* neat a tale), and I was served up my trout as an hors-d'oeuvre. Afterwards we went back to the bar and, although she favoured us both equally, Tom withdrew and, despite her protests, went up to bed.

Predictably, like a scene in *Tom Jones*, our conversation became more intimate. In the past she told me she'd had a lover who, like me, had been to Stowe (how she knew *I* had, I can't remember. Perhaps she'd asked, or I'd told her). She gave me his name and I remembered him well: an attractive but psychotic lad of the kind that old-fashioned nannies used to say were born to hang. When he left her, after a blazing and (knowing him) probably physical row, she told me he'd stolen her fur coat. I had no trouble believing her.

Gradually things became physical. I went up to bed about two a.m.

Next morning at breakfast, after our landlady, lively as ever (perhaps, given my hangover, a shade *too* lively) had brought us our bacon and eggs and left us to it, Tom raised his eyebrows in interrogation and I nodded. 'Thought it was on the cards,' he said.

There he was right, but only, in fact, in part. I'd lied. Plenty had gone on, but stopping short of what is now unattractively called 'penetration'. Not for want of trying though – the thing was, I was far too drunk (see the porter in *Macbeth*).

Tom seemed rather pleased at my 'success'. This was not

because he was vicariously lecherous, but because he felt my adventure in the small hours would in part compensate for the narrow stream, the tiny fish.

*   *   *   *   *

We left quite soon after breakfast on an affectionate note, sealed, in my case, with a kiss, and I felt even more like Henry Fielding's picaresque hero or a Rowlandson sailor. We stopped in the garden of a pub on the River Ribble outside Preston. As we drank our beer and ate some ham sandwiches I watched with fascination a young man spinning for sea-trout or salmon by casting a Devon minnow across the water. I'd seen my father spin once, and without success, on the Clwyd in spate, using a large (wooden?) reel with yards of line coiled in the grass in front of him. In theory the weight of the lure plus additional lead travelled a considerable distance, drawing the line out behind it. Then the angler wound it in again. In practice, the line often got caught up with itself, the lure was difficult to place exactly where you wanted to and sometimes caught the opposite bank, and half the time was spent correcting these failings. This young man seemed to face none of these problems. He used a fairly small metal reel of a kind unfamiliar to me, and just flicked his fairly short rod, causing the lure to fly out across the water and land exactly under the far bank with a satisfying plop. Then he reeled it in again and repeated this elegant exercise.

On enquiring, Tom explained it was a new form of reel geared not only to release line but, at a turn of the handle, to stop it dead and drop the lure into the water. I gathered that, not only had he never tried this ingenious new device, but he disapproved of it. He felt it reduced the fish's chances and the angler's skill in playing it. He was quite right on both counts, but I was intrigued by the young man's expertise.

*   *   *   *   *

When we got home Tom told me that the next time we went fishing together, he'd make sure it was on serious water with some chance of success. He could certainly afford it now. His mother had recently died in her eighties and her son, never a very astute or enthusiastic woolbroker, had inherited what was then a considerable sum of money – one hundred thousand pounds. He hinted to me that he was thinking perhaps of buying some fishing of his own.

Some months later he told me that a friend who'd stayed there warmly recommended an hotel on the River Lune near Lancaster and full of sea-trout, so he'd booked us in the following July.

Then, about three weeks before we were to set off, and completely unexpectedly, I sat with my mother in a private ward in a Liverpool nursing home and watched my father die, like his father before him, of a perforated ulcer.

A GIFT FROM TOM

M y brother was stationed abroad the night my father died, but my sister and I were in Liverpool and consumed by grief and rage. He had adored my sister Andrée, and she him. She had become a famous actress, and he took great pride in that too, but he'd have loved her just as much if she'd been an assistant librarian in Warrington.

I can't remember when and how she arrived in Liverpool that night. She was certainly not at his death-bed. But I have a short 'mental film-clip', true or not it's impossible to be sure now, of the pair of us in a Liverpool taxi on a rainy night turning the corner by a beautiful blitz-gutted Regency-Gothic church, with tears streaming down our faces. I, then as now a convinced atheist, was indulging in that most meaningless of activities, shouting abuse at a God I didn't believe existed. Andrée was repeating at intervals that if our mother had died first (she was after all eight years older than he) we'd be fighting over which of us had Tom to live with us.

Does this imply that we wouldn't be competing over my mother in this case? Yes it does, but it wasn't so much that we didn't love her, more that she drove us both mad. There was much about her that was sympathetic; I think of her now probably more often than my father, but she had a strong yet unfocused will. She was tolerant just so far as it went, but terrified of people's disapproval. She was eaten up with ambition for us, but our achievements had to be on her terms and anyway were never quite enough. It just wouldn't have done.

She was still, at sixty-eight, pretty spry, and not long afterwards left Liverpool, where she had lived all her life, and moved to Brighton. Later on, when she began to become at first confused, later seriously gaga, it was Andrée who took up the increasing burden, and there is, and always will be, a certain amount of guilt there sloshing about the sluices of my mind.

*   *   *   *   *

Maudie, though, could quite often surprise us, and her reaction to Tom's death was one such example. When her mother had died some years before, well into her eighties and still with all her marbles, Maud was swamped with grief and guilt, the latter of Jewish intensity. Yet she hadn't really liked her mother, who had bullied, mocked and made use of her all her life. Tom, who had a fairly simple view of human nature, pointed this out, which of course did the reverse of any good. 'All her drawers were in apple-pie order,' she'd say to explain her racking sobs, or she would burst into tears because, even when living for a time in reduced circumstances, her mother had never been overdrawn.

You may imagine therefore how we feared she would react to Tom's death. We braced ourselves for it and then, as so often, she surprised us. Admittedly it was a received truth that 'Maud is always good in a crisis', but it went beyond that. During those first few weeks she would pay him quiet homage – 'He was such a gentle man' – or reproach herself (unnecessarily) for rowing with him, but very rarely, over what she called 'that bloody drink'.

I am and have always been very inadequate at sensing what those around me are really feeling. I should have guessed that she had just tamped down her grief, was to mourn him desperately later and miss him constantly, for her remaining thirty years. For the moment, though, failing to read the small signs of the earthquake to come – the sudden silence of birds, the teacup rattling slightly in its saucer – I was confused, if at the same time rather impressed.

*   *   *   *   *

Then came the offer that really shook me. She knew that Tom had booked us into the fishing hotel at Hornby. It seemed a pity to cancel it. Why didn't she come with me instead – not to fish, of course? As you'd expect of me by now, I said yes immediately, but what motivated Maudie still eludes me. She would after all be sleeping in the bed *he* would have slept in, eat at the table *he* would have occupied. Was this in itself a comfort? I really don't know; but I can assure readers that, after this rather long detour, we are now back on the water.

On the appointed day I got Tom's rods, net, fishing-bag and thigh-waders (no bottle in them, alas!) out of the chest in the hall, and we set off for the hotel to arrive 'in time for luncheon' as they described it in the brochure.

The hotel itself was reassuring: slightly shabby, warm and very comfortable, with a proper pub bar (the Booth's could have stayed virgin) and 'good plain cooking'.

The owner was a shortish man, ex-military, a major, as I recall, good-mannered in an old-fashioned way, 'Dear lady' and the like, moustached and I have an impression of ginger hair, although this may be a misplaced memory of his well-worn ginger tweeds.

He also liked a drink, but stuck faithfully to Irish whiskey, a preference which, although forty years later, I now share. By the end of the evening he was always a bit tight but not at all aggressive – on the contrary, rather sentimental.

I liked him at once. I'd rung him up to explain why my mother was to replace my father.

'I'm very sad', he said to her on our arrival, 'to hear of your recent loss, dear lady.'

*　*　*　*　*

The River Lune ran across the bottom of a moderately large field at the back of the hotel. There was a long, fairly wide pool fringed by a pebble beach. The Major warned me not to disturb this during the day. If I wanted to fish in the morning or afternoon, he suggested I turn left and wade slowly down 'the flats', a half-mile or so of fairly shallow water holding rather small brown trout. This I did, and hooked several, but none worth keeping. About six I returned to the hotel as I'd been warned that dinner was held early for the convenience of those in pursuit of sea-trout, those restless silvery children of the night, whose somewhat vampiric feeding habits coincided with the appearance of the first bat.

I went up to see my mother, who was about to take a pre-prandial bath, and then went down to the bar to join the Major for 'a snort', as he called it. This, much as I enjoyed his company, was not entirely altruistic. It was because I had never fished for sea-trout and was badly in need of a few tips. Tom had done a certain amount, and if he'd been with me as intended . . . and then I suddenly realised why he wasn't. I find such little jolts one of the more distressing aspects of a recent death. How can you, even momentarily, have forgotten?

The Major was most helpful: 'Strong cast of course, at least six-pound breaking strain, extremely kind of you, no need to wade or even change your place, unlike your 'brownie' your sea-trout move all over the pool when they're on, so they'll come to you, don't strike, soft mouths you see, cheers old man, you'll pull it straight out, damn difficult *not* to strike, mind you, because they take with a great splash and tug, but try to resist it, play him like a salmon. . .' And much else, all of it to the point. My mother looked in and I left to escort her into the restaurant. I had concealed the fact that I'd still to fish for, let alone hook, a salmon. 'And flies?' I shouted over my shoulder as we moved towards a choice of consommé or shrimps from nearby Morecambe Bay. 'I'll look some out for you while you dine,' he promised and signalled yet again to the bar-man who, as though he had studied the then fashionable theory of those days 'time and motion', headed straight for the Irish optic, glass already in hand.

As we left the dining-room the Major proved to be a man of his word. 'A small selection,' he told me, handing over a little white box. 'Any of 'em will do.' And he turned back into the bar, not forgetting to ask my mother if she'd enjoyed her dinner. She said yes, and meant it. For a provincial hotel at a time when the *Good Food Guide* offered thin pickings north of Hampstead the food was excellent – not that I saw the Major himself putting it to the test.

The shadows were lengthening fast as I changed. I'd already put up my rod but, following the Major's advice, tied on a stronger leader and one of the quite large flies, a 'Black Butcher', as I subsequently learnt. I had said goodnight to Maud as I passed her room and to the Major as I'd passed the bar. In the warm light of the sun setting behind distant Lancaster, I walked across the thistled field, my shadow lengthening behind me. Along the pool, evenly spaced out at about ten-yard intervals, stood six or seven somewhat dour Lancastrians. They weren't casting yet. They were all locals, although I believe they paid the Major to fish the hotel water. I tried to launch a conversation with my nearest neighbours, 'Anything moving yet? Is it a promising evening?' But their monosyllabic reaction, 'Nay', didn't encourage me to persist. No bats yet either. But then, in the near dark, there was a heavy splash under the opposite bank and another further down the pool, and at this point the locals began to cast as one, straight ahead of them and not especially far out.

Without the Major's instruction I would have wondered why nobody dropped their fly over the individual rising fish, wouldn't have realised it was because the sea-trout were swimming rapidly and purposefully through the shallow water over the pebbled bottom hoovering up the flies and other insects as they went, while the bats, now well in evidence, skittered and banked above them like nocturnal swallows. And then, suddenly, there was a big splash and one took me. It was so unexpected I didn't strike at once, as I would have done if it had been a brownie, and by the time I reacted it had hooked itself. I'd never fought a fish in the dark before either, and it was a fair size, six pounds as it transpired; but, my heart in my mouth throughout, it yielded and, to save risking the net in the dark, I walked slowly backwards and it followed me up the shore and over the pebbles. My neighbours had reeled in when I'd hooked my fish to ensure our lines didn't get tangled, but started casting again as soon as it was clear of the water. 'It's not a bad 'un, is that,' said one of them almost warmly. I killed it with a stone, my spirits soaring, and I conceived the idea it was a gift from Tom. It was in the same spirit that, in my early days as a jazz-singer, I would appeal to the late Bessie Smith, 'Empress of the Blues', to possess me. Absurd or not, that night on the dark shore of the Lune, I felt that my father, who should of course have been casting next to me, had fulfilled his promise to give me some *real* fishing.

Even today, if there's been no action for a long time I still appeal to him, more frivolously perhaps, but not *that* much more frivolously.

*   *   *   *

Some pedants perhaps may be congratulating themselves on spotting that I've suggested that the sea-trout I caught on the Lune was my first. What of my success in Scotland, that triumphant half-hour or so which so irritated Frank Parr? Well yes, they *were* sea-trout, but comparatively small and not fished for as such either. A happy accident, and I didn't even know what they were until I'd asked. I thought, and still think, of the Hornby leviathan as my first true sea-trout. I walked back across the field to the hotel glowing with pride.

It was this euphoria which explains, although it does not excuse, what I did next. Although almost eleven p.m. I went and woke up my mother to show it to her. I never considered for a moment that she, recently widowed and not in the least interested in fishing, wouldn't share my joy. In the event, being her, not only did she not complain, but contrived to simulate rather sleepy enthusiasm. Satisfied, I went down to the bar again, handed the trout to the Major with an air of unconvincing modesty, and bought us both a final Jameson.

The following evening, our last, my hubris claimed its wages. I soon hooked another fish, played it far too roughly, and it broke me. 'You were too 'ard on 'im,' said my neighbour sounding not entirely displeased. (I discovered none of them had touched anything the previous night.)

Next day my mother and I returned, as planned, to the empty house in Liverpool and I left the following evening for a gig in Southport.

PART 2

SECOND
CHILDHOOD

5

AT HUG PUG COTTAGE

The early Sixties brought some radical changes to my life. Hoping, but with several encouraging portents, to become a full-time journalist, I left the jazz world, my first wife left me, and simultaneously I met and fell in love with Diana.

I have never planned my life, preferring to drift with the tide like an overweight jellyfish. I've trusted chance and she has seldom let me down.

For example, having just bought Diana a drink in the Colony Room under the beady eye of Muriel Belcher, I received a phone-call from my wife saying that after all she'd be unable to accompany me to the opening of 'The Establishment', London's first satirical night-club, so Diana came instead.

We finished off that night making love on Hampstead Heath (not so exclusively a gay reservation in those days). Our affair escalated, and within a very short time Victoria had moved out to join her rich lover in the flat he'd bought her in Belgravia and Diana, with her two children, one from each of her previous marriages ('Ready-Mades' I called them), had moved into the rather twee terraced cottage on Hampstead Heath.

In that these children feature, albeit marginally, in relation to fishing I shall describe them briefly. Candy, still a babe in arms, was to become a beauty later, but was a curious-looking infant. With her pendulous cheeks and slightly oriental eyes I nicknamed her 'The Japanese Warlord', although her sweet nature and habitual smile soon won her the kindlier sobriquet, 'Miss Jolly Grin-Grin'.

Poor Miss Jolly Grin-Grin had a very weak chest as a baby and toddler, and was frequently in hospital.

Candy's half-brother Patrick was six when he came to us. Since he was very young when Diana had left his father, he'd spent an unsettled childhood. Diana herself had been very young when he was born and, when pursuing her own restless life in the Chelsea set with boyfriends and trips abroad, had often dumped him with an aunt in Essex.

When she married Candy's father, a sports journalist, she proposed Patrick should come to live with them, but this too was turned down whereas I accepted. Very good-looking and extremely bright, he was, at the same time and not really surprisingly, a troubled and disruptive child.

Diana herself was plagued by insecurity, stalked by depression, and often (which I loved) a wild child. But, as I soon found out, she was also practical, competent and thoughtful. For example, once she'd taken aboard my obsession for fishing, she went out of her way to see it was available whenever possible, and not only in our halcyon days, but throughout our long life together, and even when things were going really badly. Nor had she any interest in fishing as such, although I was convinced that, once she'd tried it and for certain once she'd hooked and landed a trout, she'd share my passion – but then I have always suffered from the 'love me, love my dog' delusion.

That year, 1961, and for at least seven years after it, our life together seems to me in retrospect to have been bathed in subterranean light and, while we already shared a number of friends and acquaintances in common, she introduced me to a London as strange and diverse as a coral reef.

*   *   *   *   *

Early in 1962 Candy was seriously ill and hospitalised. The hospital was not so far from Hampstead in miles, but it took Diana over an hour each way to visit her.

My mother, following Tom's death, had moved from Liverpool to Brighton, and the first time she'd met Diana was at Euston en route.

Her initial impression: pink shoes, black fish-net stockings and tangled hair, was not favourable, but later she became very much taken with her and, when she heard about the trek involved in visiting Candy, offered to buy us a car. Diana immediately booked driving lessons and passed first time. This is absolutely typical of her powers of application. She looked at that time like the girl least likely, but she sailed through.

And so, armed with her driving licence we exchanged Maudie's cheque for a small pale green van, and Miss Jolly Grin-Grin eventually got better, if only temporarily, and returned to Hampstead.

By this time we'd begun to have au pair girls and besides Diana's mother, who adored the children and they her, was always willing, indeed eager, to baby-sit and, although this proved a grave mistake, even came to live with us for a bit. So Diana suggested we took a late honeymoon in the van – a fishing tour of Scotland.

Was this idea hers or mine? If hers it was extremely unselfish, but I suspect it wasn't, in that my parents had done exactly the same in 1925, even to the parallel indifference to fishing shared by the two women.

So we set off for the North and I'd even bought Diana her own rod, reel and waders (a complete waste of money as it transpired). It seemed a long way then – the M1 petered out before Birmingham – but eventually we crossed the border at Carlisle and aimed for Fort William, the base camp of our expedition.

Until then it all had gone well. We'd slept in B & Bs, small hotels, or sometimes on a mattress in the back of the van. I remember early one day emerging through its double doors just as the dawn mist was rising. In front of a field of ripening corn, a male pheasant strutted his gaudy stuff. It was like the first morning of the world.

But then, on the last lap of our outward expedition, a disaster took place, leading to the first real spat in our relationship, although, unlike some of our later quarrels, not very serious in the long run.

I was map-reading, never my gig, but unfortunately Diana didn't know that then. We came to a T-junction and, unaware I was reading the map upside down, I ordered a confident left turn. Several hours later, just as we should have been approaching Fort William, I saw a signpost reading Carlisle – 16 miles, and confessed. Diana, stony-faced, reversed back into a lane and drove on in complete and icy silence back along the way we'd come. To make it worse we had the car radio on because, a week or so earlier, I'd recorded a talk on Greta Garbo, who was about to be given a season of films at the National Film Theatre.

Neither of us was quite able to switch it off – that would have been an open declaration of war – but it didn't help to be sitting side by side in uncompanionable silence while my plummy voice eulogised the reclusive Swedish actress.

Eventually Diana thawed (although I was never to be trusted with the map again) and just before night fell we drove into Fort

William, and next morning set out to catch some fish, or at least I did.

*   *   *   *   *

The exact details of that holiday, even its length (a week? ten days?) are lost. Diana had of course planned it, using a book called *Where to Fish in Scotland*, and worked out the routes (she knew by then it was better to pull up to look at the map herself than to rely on me). I retain a kind of general impression of Scottish baronial hotels with antlers, scudding clouds, bracken like a rough bedspread thrown over the hills, towns of glittering granite, distant views of sullen lochs, heather the colour of bruises just beginning to fade after pub brawls, malt whisky, soft Highland voices, but comparatively little detail and certainly not in chronological order. A few events, however, remain entirely in focus. One was stopping, parched on a hot afternoon, outside a small plain isolated house on the edge of a glen. There was a sign advertising teas. We knocked. A woman, middle-aged and sour-faced, answered the door and asked us what we wanted. 'Tea,' we said. 'This is the Sabbath,' she told us icily. 'You'll get no tea from me on the Sabbath' and she banged the door in our faces.

I recall too one of our stayovers at an hotel with the mildly comic name of 'Tom Doon'. It was a dark house although not tall, full of massive Victorian furniture, and run by two old, very thin ladies whose bony fingers were permanently blue with cold. The food was spectacularly dreadful: excellent meat hideously over-cooked, indescribably water-sodden vegetables, potatoes full of eyes, but what I remember most was a huge stuffed trout on the wall of the cabbage-scented dining-room. It was indeed hardly recognisable as a trout, or at any rate some ancestor from a prehistoric era. Its body was Quasimodo-like, both saggy and humpy, but it was its great bony head which was straight out of Hieronymus Bosch. The taxidermist had given it malevolent eyes and set it with its mouth ajar to reveal an impressive number of jagged teeth. It was framed in a mahogany case and there was a small discoloured brass plaque which read 'Ferox' and gave its weight as eighteen pounds and its place of capture as Tom Doon itself, in 1933.

It was a still but dark day as we pushed off (Diana reading) into the comparatively small loch, reed-edged, below the hotel, and with dark and peaty water suggesting great depth. I caught nothing, there were no rises, but all the time I was imagining the huge monster of the glass case eyeing, with baleful malevolence, my fly as I cast and retrieved, and then slowly but deliberately rising to take it.

I hadn't read Ted Hughes's *Pike* at that time; indeed it hadn't long been published, but when I did, several years later, I recognised his sense of awe, of fear and desire, and I was back again on the dark waters of Tom Doon.

But silently cast and fished
With the hair frozen on my head
For what might move, for what eye might move
The still splashes on the dark pond,

Owls hushing the floating woods
Frail on my ear against the dream
Darkness beneath night's darkness had freed,
That rose slowly towards me, watching.'

Perhaps a Ferox did rise and watch, but if so that's all it did. In fact I caught no trout at all at Tom Doon, nor that many elsewhere.

Calling in at Hardy's a few days ago (one of the few sentences that give me undiluted snobbish pleasure) I asked, while they were fetching two rods I'd had repaired, what they knew of Ferox. Not that much it turned out. But, whereas in the nineteenth and early twentieth century it was thought of as a separate species, it was now believed to be a regular trout modified by opportunism, environment and longevity. Nor is its size quite so impressive. In the lakes stocked by fish-farms they often introduce specially bred and enormous brownies or rainbows. I've never landed one but I've hooked a few and one, on quite a small stretch of water, stripped off all my line up to the backing, which of course, being old, snapped at once.

So I didn't learn much about the monster of Tom Doon,

bought some black gnats, dark olives and a new Hardy's product to prolong the surface life of dry flies and emerged into the drizzle of Pall Mall.

*   *   *   *   *

Back in Scotland almost forty years ago, I was fishing an estuary pool as the light was dying. Suddenly, without premonition, a big sea-trout, presumably swimming upriver on the tide, took so unexpectedly that I didn't strike and it hooked itself. Grassed and dispatched, Diana and I returned to the van only to find that, due I suppose to the encroaching sea, it was sinking into the boggy turf. Diana, admirably unfazed, tried to move it, but the wheels spun round in a flurry of mud, every revolution digging us in deeper. Luckily we found a helpful farmer and as it was not the Sabbath (no fishing then anyway in Scotland or Wales), and as he was clearly rather taken with Diana, he fetched his tractor and pulled us free.

Driving back to the hotel, our pretty green van looking like a hippo after a good wallow, I looked at the sea-trout on the net beside me. It seemed, in the light of our near-disaster, to have grown smaller.

*   *   *   *   *

One day, however, shines out from that holiday, one of those rare events to restore the angler's faith, not only at the time but for many years ahead. It was furthermore a repetition of that miraculous afternoon some five years earlier when I was still a touring jazz singer. Again the young sea-trout (average weight one-and-a-half pounds) ran upriver snapping at everything like cheerful suicides. In no time they were on almost every other cast and it occurred to me that, if I were to hand the rod over to Diana, the battle with a fighting fish or two would surely convert her, teach her to cast, resolve my slight, very slight, guilt, at expecting her to cater for my obsession despite her total indifference to its cause.

Two casts later there was a fish on and I handed over the twitching, bucking rod. She raised the tip and played it to the manner born.

Several times she completed this exercise and then a very tall, exquisitely polite man in breast-waders, and his equally tall son, approached us and asked us if we would mind leaving the pool as they were about to fish it down for salmon. I suspected it was his water anyway and he could have been dismissive or dictatorial, was perhaps the local laird (the English accent no encumbrance here. Most of the *really* posh Scotsmen I've met neither rolled their Rs nor used the word 'wee'). Anyway the dozen sea-trout made it perfectly easy to concede our place with a good grace. I said I hoped we hadn't disturbed 'the fish' (fish means salmon only in Scotland, although, in retrospect, I'm not sure if this applied to ex-Etonian lairds), and we drove off.

In the van, our catch was to feed the whole hotel that evening; I said nothing, expecting Diana to announce her total conversion, but she remained silent. At last, unable to bear it any longer, I asked her outright. How had she enjoyed landing those hard-fighting beautiful silvery fish? It was fine, she told me, very enjoyable. Did that mean, I quizzed her, that she now understood the *point* of fishing, might indeed take it up? Certainly not, she said. If every time you went out you were sure to catch all those sea-trout perhaps, but of course you couldn't be sure, on the contrary most often you caught nothing . . .

So that was that, and from that day on Diana has neither picked up a rod nor cast a fly. Not once!

*   *   *   *   *

We made love a lot on that holiday, once on the side of a steep hill overlooking a loch with a tall castle built out on an isthmus directly below us. I think it's the castle reproduced on lots of Scottish tourist board posters – very like, anyway.

The hill was so steep I had to wedge the heel of my wader against the trunk of a rowan tree. I like to believe – the dates are about right – that our son Tom was conceived on that hillside.

The night before we were to drive south again I woke with a terrible burning in my throat and chest. I'd convinced myself by dawn that it was lung cancer, but then I remembered that a night or two earlier at dinner I'd swallowed a small roast potato whole.

Comparatively cold on the outside, it was piping hot inside and had burst on the way down, infecting my whole windpipe. Back in London a short course of antibiotics soon put paid to it.

I mention this far from riveting incident only because of a curious parallel with my father. On his way north for *his* fishing honeymoon, he and my mother stayed the night in Coniston where an elderly relative, Cousin Emma, had a house. There was no question of them leaving next day. Tom had developed a quinsy, a painful boil *in the throat*, for which the only cure is to wait until it bursts. This took several days; his mother came up to help look after him. (Maud said later, 'If anyone had seen me and my mother-in-law walking in the fields they'd have thought the marriage was in trouble already!') Eventually it burst. Relief is apparently instant, and they set off next day.

They spent the night in Carlisle. In the lobby was an envelope stuck in the green baize letter rack. It was addressed to 'Thomas Quinsy Esq.' and my father, concluding it to be an irritating laddish joke, tore it into fragments. It turned out, however, there *was* a real Thomas Quinsy staying in the hotel!

*   *   *   *   *

In 1962 I returned to the fishing hotel in Hornby, Lancs, this time in celebration instead of mourning. We took the children too, Paddy and Miss Jolly Grin-Grin both, the latter at that point well.

The dear Major, several crates of Jameson's emptied since my last visit, greeted me warmly ('How's your dear mother?') and welcomed Diana and the kids. Candy demonstrated immediately the aptness of her nickname; Paddy glared suspiciously.

We weren't given a room or rooms in the hotel but lodged in a very pretty cottage in the grounds, although of course we ate in the main building. During that period Diana and I were very 'touchy-feely' as the Americans rather repellently put it, and Paddy had, I felt, very mixed feelings about it. On the one hand it suggested we wouldn't break up, or not yet anyway; on the other it demonstrated a certain exclusivity which might, and he was a master at testing us, exclude him. On this holiday, though, he was, in the main, at his sunniest and most lovable.

He always had a somewhat disconcerting instinct for nicknames – he called the psychologist he was to attend later for several fruitless years 'Miss Horrible-Horrible'. At Hornby he called our detached quarters 'Hug-Pug Cottage'. It stuck immediately. When Diana was looking out fishing photographs for this book she came across several of Paddy on this holiday. Without thinking about it, she identified them on the mount: 'at Hug Pug '62'.

The major took an avuncular interest in us all. I suspect he'd put us in Hug Pug for the sake of the largely elderly and rather conventional guests, but he knew we'd enjoy it more too.

One evening, when I dropped into the bar for a nightcap on my way back from losing several sea-trout, I found him alone, seemingly lonely and glad of the company. He'd sent the barman to bed and was helping himself. 'Tell me,' he asked me out of the blue and quite seriously, 'are you married to that beautiful young woman?' 'No,' I said, puzzled as to his motive. Was he about to order us to leave? Was he going to launch into a series of 'Nudge, nudge' jokes? Happily, neither. 'I didn't think so,' he said, his tone neither conspiratorial nor disapproving. I think his object was to tell me he knew but didn't mind. He was a thoroughly decent old toper.

It was he too who suggested Paddy might enjoy coarse fishing off a rocky promontory under some cliffs about a hundred yards from the hotel. There was a variety of coarse fish in the Lune: perch, tench, roach, eels and others, and he had a rod, reel, weights and a float. He'd point out to me where to dig up worms.

Next day he was as good as his word and Paddy, touched perhaps by his interest, managed to show some enthusiasm. It was justified too. After half an hour I spent with him he'd grasped all the principles and caught enough to keep him interested.

Then, one afternoon, there was a disaster and a row. I've never worked out what exactly motivated him or irritated me to quite the extent it did. What happened was this. The weather had been fine but quite suddenly, when Paddy was seated on his rock, it clouded over and began to pour down, the kind of rain that is on the point of becoming hail, rain with an edge of malice.

I walked over to him from where I'd been casting on 'the Flats' downriver for trout, to go back to Hug Pug together. There would be a hot bath, some tea and biscuits, I promised, but he sat there, already soaking wet, as immobile and silent as a figure in a fountain. Finally, increasingly exasperated, I dragged him to his feet, picked up the rod which he'd dropped on purpose, and we set off, he requiring some manhandling, towards the welcoming cottage windows. We were half way there when he pulled his next trick. Slipping from my grasp, he quite deliberately sank to the sodden ground, stuck his thumb in his mouth, and curled up in the embryo position. The rain hammered down more relentlessly than ever and I, consumed with helpless rage, yelled like King Lear in the storm scene.

How did it end? Did I half-drag, half-carry him back? Did Diana come out and persuade him – she had always more authority with the children than I? Did he suddenly rise to his feet and walk back unaided? In a way this would have been most typical. I've no recollection of calming down, of a truce or a peace. I feel still I behaved badly in screaming at him. I've never 'solved' this incident. Yesterday, fishing the gentle Lambourne, there was just such an instant, short-lived downfall. Without waterproof clothing and a fair way from the hut, I stuck it out, thinking of course of Paddy and his sodden despair thirty-eight summers ago.

It didn't put him off fishing, however, neither then nor, although it never became a passion, later. I'd hopes, though. I thought, with encouragement, it might turn into an addiction. It never did, though – not fishing.

* * * * *

The year after 1963, the Beatles in ascension, Tom born and toddling in dungarees, Diana hired a cottage in Pembrokeshire (Sir Benfro). With three children it must have been quite large, although as 'the fittings and furnishings' were purely functional I can only remember the kitchen and especially the old sink with its slate slab just inside the back door.

Just outside the back door was certainly one reason, perhaps the main reason, why Diana booked the cottage. Behind a fairly low brick wall, a couple of yards beyond the building and running parallel to it, was a trout stream. 'Trout stream' is a loose term, and in this case it would have been fruitless to sue our landlords for misrepresentation; a stream it was – just, minuscule trout it contained. It trickled past on the other side of the wall. Diana had, however, checked up that there was other available club water in the area. Meanwhile it was quite fun for Paddy and me to catch the tiddlers on a very light cast and the smallest 'drab little thing' in my fly-box, and they were delicious eating.

One day Diana encountered a mystery. Five little trout had been taken from the fridge, laid out in a straight row on the slate slab and individually wrapped from the neck down in small slices of bacon. Candy, it transpired, was responsible. The trout, she explained, were in hospital, a setting she knew only too well. It was less funny than sad.

One morning Paddy, in a state of high excitement, ran into the cottage to tell me there were two huge eels in the stream. He was right and they *were* big too! So we put a worm on the hook and dropped it in the water and immediately one of the cool, demonic creatures took it, jerked its serpentine head and instantly snapped the cast. We changed to a stronger cast, a larger hook. The other eel took that. This time it wasn't able to break the leader in midstream so it swam into a kind of cave on the far bank and used the purchasing power of its retreat to effect its freedom and thereby throwing Paddy, who was using all his strength, flat on his back.

Without much hope now, for both eels had hooks in their mouths and would, you'd have thought, have become a tad suspicious of worms dangled in front of them on a perfectly visible leader, we tied on a salmon fly of my father's stripped of its feathers and joined by a hawser-like leader to the line. Threading on a gargantuan worm, we lobbed it gently over the low brick wall and, as soon as it hit the water, one of the eels took it.

It aimed straight for its cave among the boulders, but this time everything held and, after what seemed like an hour but was probably five minutes, it gave in and, such was the pressure we had on, flew out of the water and landed, coiling and thrashing, on the pebbled verge between the cottage and the low brick wall. Paddy danced with glee. When we looked again the other eel had made itself scarce.

*   *   *   *   *

Of all river fish the eel is the least pleasant to land and the most difficult, however humane its would-be executioner, to kill. Also, with the exception of the genuinely diabolic lamprey, the most sinister; a snakelike fish, mysterious in its breeding habits, in its unpiscine inability to drown in the air. None of these characteristics touched Paddy that morning. This was *his* eel.

It performed its repertoire of tricks: covering the net with slime, coiling itself up the line, making it almost impossible to dislodge the hook and then, despite our liberal application of the priest, rigorous writhing. At last however, although even then managing the occasional convulsion, it was to all intents and purposes dead, and Diana took a photograph of her proud and beaming son, rod in his left hand, the eel suspended from his right. Later we ate it, stewed in milk – it was delicious!

*   *   *   *   *

On that holiday I joined a fishing club and each day was dropped at the River Teifi unaware, until the next year, that it was a sewin river ('sewin' is Welsh for sea-trout, usually described as 'salmon-trout' by fishmongers and the non-angling public and, except when running in young schools as on those two occasions in Scotland, best fished for at dusk or in the night. That year, though, through ignorance, I fished in the day and caught very small brown trout, although apparently there were bigger ones up nearer the source. Indeed it's very possible that the small brown trout I caught *were* potential sewin. Sewin, sea-trout, salmon-trout, call them what you will, are not a separate species like salmon, but brown trout who decide to go to sea for a year or two before returning up their rivers to spawn. 'Salmon-trout' is therefore, although fishermen scorn its use, an appropriate description – they are trout which behave like salmon. They don't migrate so far, though. Salmon swim up towards the Arctic to feed and grow. Sea-trout hang around the local estuary. Once it was discovered *where* the salmon went, the commercial netting started. No wonder the salmon is a threatened species, the gap filled with those poor grey tasteless ghosts of the loch farms.

Various theories exist, usually to do with the chemical make-up of the water, as to why some rivers have no sea-trout, others some runs, varying from regular to occasional, while others yet again hold nothing but sea-trout, although they often coexist with salmon. The Teifi and its near neighbour, the Towy, hold salmon and sea-trout only, plus, naturally, various coarse fish. I persisted, however, in fishing every day and I knew no one up until then to consult.

One lunchtime Diana and the kids rattled down in the van to pick me up. They found me all right and suddenly Candy (two? three?) ran up to me and bit me very hard on the admittedly quite prominent stomach. It really hurt, and almost drew blood. I yelped with pain.

Diana sternly, although even I could see there was some-thing gratuitously comic about such an inexplicable act, asked what she meant by it. Candy's answer was perfectly logical. Diana had told her they were going to 'meet Georgie'. Candy had taken it to be 'meat', and what do you do to meat? You bite it.

* * * * *

On the last day of the holiday we went to pay the owner of the cottage. He was a farmer called Mr James. The farm was at the far end of a long, straight, slightly ascending lane and cupped in hills. Mr James had a round bespectacled wife whom we were soon to meet, and four children we didn't get to know until later. The farm was a red brick, late Victorian building, a dairy herd the heart of its economy. Quite rare for Wales, Welsh was their first language. You could tell by the construction of certain sentences.

Mr James was a sturdy rubicund figure. While paying him, we told him how we'd fallen in love with the area and were thinking of looking for a cottage. Mr James said he had an empty cottage quite near the farm but didn't want to sell it. Diana, who is much better than I at understanding what people are *really* saying, knew immediately he *would* sell at the right price. She'd also been keeping her eyes open at what they were asking for cottages in Cardiganshire and Pembrokeshire (aka Sir Benfro, whom I always imagined as a knight out of the *Alice* books; not the gentle White Knight but a creature both more aggressive and ridiculous – one of the Tweedle brothers perhaps, as dressed by Alice for battle in kitchen utensils). Of course at some point between then and now they changed the names of all the Welsh counties to legendary heroes, although whether this was to placate nationalism, or because they were doing much the same thing in England I don't know. Perhaps now they'll change them back, or not.

At all events Diana had paused to look in the windows of High Street estate agents and the crammed columns of local newspapers and knew pretty accurately what the sort of cottage we were looking for was worth – less, she discovered, than modern bungalows. Also, she asked herself, why was Mr James taking us to see the cottage that was 'not for sale'?

So Mr James turned right in front of his austere farmhouse and up a narrow and rougher lane at right angles to that leading to the main road five hundred yards away. There were trees and lush high summer vegetation and the chirruping and scraping of birds and insects, all of which led me into playing a childish game in my head which still, given the right stimulation, sometimes fills my mind, although most often when wading up a weedy creek under thick foliage. It's called 'Up the Amazon'.

After running in a vaguely straight line, the lane bent to the left, crossed an old bridge (it would need repairing later) and then climbed a short but abrupt hill and there, on a small plateau, a forested valley behind it leading steeply down to another tiny stream and behind that a hill, an overgrown kitchen garden in front of it and beyond that fields (one full of Mr James's fat pink pigs) leading to the main road to Cardigan, was 'Gaer', a beautiful old stone cottage.

In front of it a small garden. Inside a slate floor and a fairly small sitting-room with a staircase leading up to the two bedrooms above, and behind a large kitchen, almost barnlike, with a huge walk-in fireplace. To the right of the sitting-room was a small, quite well-lit study, or so I marked it down in my head. There was an outside stone privy and no kitchen – that would have to be built on later – only, I suddenly remembered, it was not for sale.

Returning to the farm, Diana managed to get me on one side and told me to offer one thousand eight hundred pounds, more than would have been offered on the open market. I waited until we were just getting into the van and then said that 'if at any time he changed his mind. . .' The sum seemed to electrify him as with a cattle-prod. He offered us a cup of tea. We could hear him saying something in Welsh. While we were eating delicious scones and Welsh cakes – Mrs James was an excellent pastrycook – Mr James accepted our proposal as it would enable him to build a milking parlour. There was no problem with searches, surveys and lawyers and quite soon Gaer was ours.

6

PASSING THE TEST

At the other end of the lane which led up to the James's farm was a tiny hamlet, Pen-y-Bryn. There were very few houses, a garage, a handsome neo-classical chapel and a pub, the Pen-y-Bryn Arms. The garage belonged to the pub, which meant at times a great deal of honking was necessary when you wanted filling up. The pub itself (where that particular failing never applied) faced the chapel like an illustration of the Broad and Narrow Ways.

Old Nick's earthly rep in this case was a short, hedgehog-like man, fond of his own merchandise and known, as is so often the case in nickname-loving Wales, as either Dai Pen-y-Bryn, Dai Neverclosed, or most often Dai Faircop. He'd gained this last when discovered by the police (not the local force: they'd never have touched him without advance warning, but a raiding party from Swansea) drawing a pint for a customer at two a.m. and, when asked for an explanation, came out with this traditional owning up to wrongdoing.

His wife, a very bright and highly educated woman, tended to operate like a Greek Chorus when it came to describing her old man's behaviour pattern. 'He's getting up,' she'd say at midday and indeed immediately you'd hear his feet thump on the linoleum above the bar, 'and now he's sitting on the bed weeping remorsefully.' She would also refer to him most of the time as 'The Entertainment'.

Rumour had it that, in her youth, she had been a mistress of Augustus John, a perfectly possible if hardly unique position.

When we first moved to Wales it was entirely dry on the Sabbath, but then a county-by-county referendum took place and whereas Cardiganshire elected to remain dry, Pembrokeshire went wet and the Pen-y-Bryn Arms was not only on the drinking side of the border but furthermore the first pub available; so, like invaders, locals and tourists streamed in.

You might have thought Dai Faircop would have been pleased, but on the contrary. . .

Before, if you'd wanted a drink on Sunday morning, you knocked on the back door. From then on, if prepared to face being in trouble when you got home, the dinner ruined, you could stay as long as you liked; the secrecy compensated for having to keep the noise down and a complete if voluntary ban on that wonderful

Fishermen All

Above left: My mother and father in the '20s in fancy dress.

Above right: My father, I would guess in his early '30s.

Below: My paternal Grandfather, a Territorial Officer in the last century.

Above: Great uncle Willie in fancy dress, before his stroke. After it he unselfishly rented fishing and shooting for the benefit of his family.

Top left: 'Hooked' at a young age, Coniston – the first known shot of me fishing (for Perch).

Top right: My father, me and Bill, Coniston.

Above: Paddy proudly displays his triumphant catch - an enormous eel caught on holiday in Pembrokeshire.

Above: Like father like stepson. With Paddy at 'Hug Pug', Hornby Lancashire, 1962.

Above: Paddy fishing at Hornby.

Left: 'Miss Jolly Grin Grin', alias the 'Japanese War Lord', 1963. And with mum, **Below**.

Above: 'Gaer', our first cottage, near Cardigan.

Above: Tom, Candy and Paddy bringing home our family supper in Scotland.

Right: A rare Salmon (for me) caught at the Tower in Late August.

Right: Salmon and sea trout caught on the river Spey, Scotland in the '60s.

Below: My first trout after buying a mile of the River Usk in 1983.

Right: Almost a gentleman, Wales 1983.

Left: They're just not on, for some reason.

Below: Outside the Tower with my unimpressed step-granddaughter Kezzie Moynihan.

Below: Fighting a rather small salmon in Russia, in the '70s.

Left: In Watamu, Kenya – '90s with sail fish, January 1999.

Above left: At Hemingways, Watamu Kenya with sail fish and assorted catch, January 1999.

Above Right: Weighing in at Hemingways.

Right: Memento of the 132 lbs striped marlin, tagged and released.

Perhaps the very next cast...

choral singing that takes over the Welsh in their cups. All the regulars were there every Sunday including a much-admired figure; a handsome, gypsy-like man with moleskin trousers, boots, an earring and an open shirt with a red scarf at the throat, who was said to have fathered most of the children thereabouts.

But with the lifting of the ban there was little room for the locals until after closing time at two p.m. and that was somehow not the same thing at all.

'They swim in, them tourists,' said Dai Neverclose gloomily, 'buy half a pint of shandy and nurse it until closing time. Taking up good drinking men's space,' he grumbled. 'Half a pint of bloody shandy!'

He was right, of course, although I did rather enjoy the tight-mouthed faces of the chapel-goers emerging from 'Syon' (or whatever it was called) at the exact moment Dai Pen-y-Bryn unlatched his front door.

*   *   *   *   *

Separating the façades of both pub and place of worship was the main road. Standing at Dai's door, to the right it led to innumerable small towns and villages whose names, as Jonathan Miller once pointed out, look as if they were made up from the letters left over in 'Scrabble'. If you turned left, however, in three or four miles you reached the outskirts of Cardigan itself.

It was an ancient and interesting town and not so big that

you couldn't stand almost anywhere within its boundaries and see the surrounding countryside. It relied in part on tourists but, at any rate during the middle Sixties, not excessively so. The high street accommodated national chains like Boots and W. H. Smith, but also local shops – Morgan's, Evans's, Price's, Jones's etc. There were banks, men's outfitters, dry cleaners, and of course pubs – many of them.

Of these we favoured The Black Lion, a fairly large house run by a plump eccentric Englishman called Aspinal, whose appearance and irritability were reminiscent of Evelyn Waugh. He had a sharp-tongued wife and a daughter who was pretty if, perhaps, rather over-aware of it.

When we first arrived, on a shelf above the bar, Frank had a display of those screw-top vacuum jars designed to preserve fruit. He used them, however, to hold his collection of animal shit, not ordinary animals, of course, like cows or sheep, but rare creatures, aardvarks or hyenas, all carefully labelled. He offered no explanation for this scatological pursuit, nor was he willing to divulge his sources. Once, however, I spotted him in another pub in conversation with a man I knew to be the owner-cum-ringmaster of a small family circus playing the town. I was also aware, from an enjoyable visit with Diana and the kids the night before, that it boasted a performing seal.

One lunchtime Frank, who had a bit of a crush on Diana, led her round the pub introducing her to the locals. After he'd been ordered back behind the bar by his irritated wife, one of the farmers she'd just met told Diana that she had just witnessed Frank playing his favourite game. 'What's that?' she asked.

With that slow, rather beautiful, clearly enunciated delivery used to indicate a dismissive critical judgement of the English, he told her, 'Getting on well with the Welsh.'

I've spent a fair proportion of the last thirty years in Wales and I still find the Welsh mysterious. Certainly, and for good historical reasons, they mistrust the English in general, and it takes a certain time for them to lower the drawbridge, but personally I experienced very little aggression and much kindness, although appearing on telly-welly may have helped initially. What I *did* find rare, though, was the Welsh equivalent of 'Uncle Tom' ('Uncle Dai', perhaps), the fawning, sly, forelock-tugging stereotype of English prejudice. Of course, like all stereotypes, they exist. In Cardigan it was the owner of the tackle-shop.

Several years after we'd been at Gaer, he'd somehow come to believe that I had been knighted.

At the start of the next season, and in need of sewin flies, I braced myself against the normal outburst of sycophancy, only to be knocked flying by a tidal wave of writhing congratulations: 'So I hear Her Majesty has dubbed you a knight and, with all due respect to her, not before time. Sir George Melly, is it now? Well, Sir George, and what can we do for you? What are your current requirements, Sir George . . .?' He rolled the title round his tongue as if it were coated with honey or molasses.

Eventually I managed to disabuse him of the idea (it may

have originated in *Private Eye*) but, although disappointed, he soon put a brave face on it.

'You deserve it,' he said, as if to buck me up after my disappointment. 'Oh yes, you *thoroughly* deserve it, and it will come. Yes indeed!'

I didn't have the heart to convince him that the last thing I wanted or would accept was a tap on the shoulder by the grumpy queen of an evaporating empire.

*   *   *   *   *

Not long after buying Gaer I discovered my friend Alun Owen, ex-actor, highly regarded TV playwright, lived nearby.

He was indeed, as his name suggests, half Welsh, although, when in Wales, more Welsh than the Welsh (note the alliteration – a national characteristic). Basically, though, like myself, he was a Liverpudlian and, much to the irritation of Diana, who has always detested Scouse chauvinism, we spent a lot of time inventing and elaborating a Merseyside mythology centred on an attractive, if outrageous, slapper called Norma, and her two obsessed but appalled suburban admirers, who spoke in the refined tones of Paul McCartney and hoped to be taken for posh.

Alun was central to my daytime life. Diana, the kids and I drove over many Sunday mornings to join him, his smiling wife Mary and their two sons on the veranda of the solid Victorian house a mile outside the town. I hear still, in the mind's ear, the tonic fizzing over the ice cubes bobbing about in the huge gins.

Alun and I met most days in The Lion and behaved badly when drunk at village fêtes. We behaved well, though, one evening when, cheerfully abandoning my fishing, we sat together to watch the film he'd scripted, the Beatles' *A Hard Day's Night*. It was shown, at Alun's request, the same night as its simultaneous première in Liverpool and Leicester Square.

I am always reminded (O Alun and your proud family, beware the sword of Damocles) of that night, those summers, when I hear or think of the haunting lines from a pop song of the period,

Those were the days my friend
We thought they'd never end.

*   *   *   *   *

Life at the cottage was idyllic, and most afternoons, when Diana and the kids drove down to the beaches, I sat, rattling with pep pills, already illegal but supplied by a sympathetic GP, struggling with my first book, *Owning Up*, a memoir of the previous decade. Sometimes, though, I'd go with them, down twisting lanes, a honk needed on every corner, past useless signposts, their destinations smeared in green paint by the Welsh Nationalists, to the towering cliffs, bird-loud, with the seal-haunted waters below; steep paths leading down to half-moons of yellow sand and huge rocks like ossified monsters rearing up out of the sea beyond.

Diana and I did a lot of junk-shopping too (there was even a magic shed on one of the more accessible beaches), and we needed furniture because there was now not only the cottage, that actually needed very little, but, with the radical need to change life which is at the centre of her being, we had just sold the Hampstead cottage and moved into a big house in Camden Town. Happily in the mid-Sixties second-hand furniture, china, etc. was still absurdly cheap. Over and over again we loaded up the van.

* * * * *

Emerging from the James's lane, turning neither right towards Scrabbleland nor left to Cardigan, was a fairly kempt B-road leading, in half a mile, to the considerable village of Kilgerran. It had a ruined castle, a general grocer (Mr Pope), a pretty pub, some old cottages and a rash of new bungalows in the Welsh taste, but it also boasted a quite substantial, state-of-the-art public lavatory. Tom was in no doubt as to his preferences in Kilgerran – Mr Pope's and the gents.

On the left, below the castle, flowed the River Towy on its way to the sea. There are cliffs and woods on the far side, but on the Kilgerran bank a flat area, a useful platform for the spectators, judges and committee of the annual coracle festival (the coracle is a prehistoric boat made from skins stretched over a wicker framework. It is almost circular and very difficult to handle with its one paddle). The festival included boat races, swimming races (comparatively dangerous, as the river there is quite fast) and finally, a not very convincing simulation of the netting of an obviously dead salmon and the greeting of this charade with fake whoops of triumph. If all salmon had to be netted from coracles there'd be no world-wide crisis, no need for fish farms, or, increasingly, catch and return.

Leave Kilgerran behind you, drive along the winding road to Kennath Falls, and en route the river offers pool after pool, many of them belonging to the Cardigan Angling Association. Sometimes the road runs parallel with the water, sometimes you glimpse it from above, on hills with dog-loud farms, while crossing the old bridges, but you are never very far from it. In time I got to know these pools, each very different in atmosphere, some across a single field, some below a thick steep wood, some skirting industrial buildings, others primeval in feeling. I would choose which to fish each night, but if I caught a sewin at a certain pool (not all that common an event) I'd tend to return there for several evenings running. Some sewin fanatics fish all night, crawling into a sleeping-bag for the dead hours between nocturnal rises. I never went so far as that. I'd hit the water about six-thirty to seven p.m., depending on sundown, and then return to the cottage – around midnight after the first rise was over and I knew that however late I packed it in I could always get a drink at Dai Neverclose.

Was Diana still willing to drive me to the fishing, to wait or return for me when I'd finished? She was not! Quite early on in

Pembrokeshire she gave me an ultimatum. I must learn to drive myself.

There was no question, I told her, of a car, like a surprising number of my exact contemporaries, I have never even contemplated driving a car. My reasons? Too fond of drink? Lack of empathy with machinery? A low macho count? Snobbish irritation at those who bask in their reflection in the gleaming panelling of what they tend to call 'a lot of motor'?

As for a motor-bike? Worse! The very idea made me turn pale. (I've, much later in life, had two crushes on women who drove powerful bikes, both of them dressed in black leather. One was a White Witch from Lancashire, the other a young Essex Lesbian, but even then I was in no way tempted to follow in their tyre-tracks.)

Diana let me ramble on hysterically in this vein, but then, when I'd finally finished, mentioned the word 'bicycle'. This produced equally fervent objections, but for exactly the opposite reasons. How could she expect me, in my flabby condition, to pedal several miles in hilly country, loaded with a rod, net, and fishing bag? And as to cycling back in the dark! Out of the question! I was no longer young either – I was nearly forty!

There was no solution. I should either have to give up fishing or move to where it was in walking distance.

She asked me, finally, if I had ever heard of a 'Solex'. I hadn't. She told me it was a mechanically assisted bicycle with an engine housed in a small circular drum at the front. When we got back to London in a fortnight's time she had arranged for me to try one. Meanwhile, of course, she would continue to drive me . . .

This whole conversation exactly confirms Diana's view of me as instantly in opposition to any innovation in my life she might propose, however advantageous. As she is, by temperament, the exact opposite, this can lead to minor confrontations, although she always wins and is usually right.

At the great cycle shop in Kentish Town, I was an instant Mr Toad-like convert to the 'Solex'. Here was the key to my piscatorial freedom.

At dinner that night I sat next to an elderly queen who lived most of the time in Provence. Naturally I was full of my new toy. 'Ah, a Solex,' he said wistfully, 'every French teenager's dream.' It was French then? Even better, although in reality I looked more like a governess than a teenage frog as I put-putted along the lanes of Pembrokeshire. Indeed, later on a friend of mine, meeting me mounted, after a very severe haircut, christened me 'Sister George', but by the time this happened it was even more appropriate for I had graduated to a moped – a Maxi-Putsch – and remained faithful to this two-stroke enabler for the next thirty years. How I was emboldened to make the change I can't remember. Perhaps I was simply seduced by the chrome, the scarlet or purple bodywork.

* * * * *

There was one more obstacle to overcome before I could take full advantage of my territorial freedom. On both Solex and Maxi-Putsch you had to wear a learner's sign, back and front, until you'd passed the driving test and I feared that, if I never got through, I might be considered so feeble and hopeless as to be permanently barred.

This may have been paranoia, perhaps mischievously fanned by Diana, but failing my test *four times* didn't help!

Here is how.

First: misjudged distance between Camden Town and Hendon. In consequence ten minutes late. Test cancelled.

Second: I arrogantly hadn't felt it necessary to do more than glance at the Highway Code, and that commonsense was enough. I was wrong.

Third: This happened the day after I graduated from the French teenagers' dream to the West London's mod's necessity. If the Solex wouldn't start through pedalling, I'd climb off and push it vigorously back and forth a few times which usually did the trick. When the moped refused to come to life, I applied the same remedy, failing to realise how much more powerful the new scooter was. It shot forward and ran over the examiner's foot.

'Reason for failure,' he wrote standing on one leg (for they are not allowed to tell you, but could mark your card), 'insufficient control of vehicle.'

Fourth: I just, but only just, avoided running down an

examiner (not mine) who had stepped out from between two cars to test his applicant's braking reactions. Unfortunately my man saw this happen.

I began to become obsessed with Hendon, convinced they saw me coming and sneered in anticipation. I was depressed too by their stony-faced lack of humour and it seemed to me they were infected by both the accent and attitudes of the nearby Hendon Police College. I started to think I'd never pass and then Diana suggested, quite casually, that I try Wales. It worked instantly. The examiner was a twinkly, middle-aged man who mentioned immediately that apparently I drank in his uncle's pub.

Given this information I felt quite relaxed and, to remove any suspicion of nepotic bias on the part of my examiner, I had by now learnt something from my mistakes in tight-arsed Hendon. He passed me, and the first thing I did, before going round for a celebratory drink at his uncle's, was to remove the shabby 'L' signs and dump them in a municipal litter-bin before performing a Native American dance around it!

*   *   *   *   *

My intention, when I started this chapter, was to write a short preamble to my nights by the water, but somehow it has spread itself, and by now seems to have become a chapter in itself. I don't feel guilty about this, nor will it be the only time during this book when I walk away from the riverbank for a few pages. I own several

T-shirts with, printed on the front, the image of a fish, fly or lure, and above it the legend

LIFE IS FISHING
and in smaller letters
THE REST IS JUST DETAILS

I think this is an overstatement. Except for purely instructional manuals ('How to improve your casting', that kind of thing) to write of one's life in waders as though it took place in a vacuum would be a chilly undertaking. Nor do any of the angling writers I admire and enjoy subscribe to it. Although I may be more self-indulgent than most. I shall continue, anyhow, to place my time by the river within the wider context of my life, however broadly brushed in.

Meanwhile, every evening during those distant summers, I'd mount my Solex and set out to try my luck. Beneath the water, holed up among the roots of trees, the sewin waited for dusk.

7

THE WEST YET GLIMMERS

There were at least six pools on the Teifi in which I could and did fish regularly, but I was most successful in, and therefore visited most often, the long stretch below the small 'modernistic' industrial building whose function (generator? pumping station?) I never established and lacked the curiosity to find out. Surrounded by meadows, backed by woods, it reminded me, because of its odd proportions and incongruous situation, of an element in a collage or the factory across the Seine in Seurat's *Bathers*.

Leaving my Solex, later on my scooter, chained up by a five-barred gate, I ploughed through tall and tangled grass towards the water. If there was no wind the air was punctuated by clouds of midges (perhaps it was they who turned my thoughts to

Seurat). Naturally I wore insect-repellent, although I'm not of especial interest to these 'small, two-winged flies of which the female has a blood-sucking proboscis' (Fowler's Dictionary), these microscopic Draculas. Yet even at their least aggressive they're a nuisance, and I've known those for whom they are a true menace. I have watched two people walking side by side at evening, one entirely visible, the other a blurred cloud. I've always been intrigued, however, to realise that each of these tiny creatures, several of whom could gather, like medieval angels, on the head of a pin, have every one of them an individual brain, containing at any rate a few encoded instructions: hatch, swarm, sting and drink blood (if female), mate and die. Midges do vary from place to place. I've never had much trouble in Wales. Scottish midges are far more aggressive, but the worst in my experience are Irish. On the banks of a loch in Donegal I was two or three times forced to run for it or go mad.

*　*　*　*　*

With my fishing bag slung over my shoulder, my telescopic net tucked into the strap, thigh-waders, an ancient tweed cap which had once belonged to Great-Uncle Willy, dead those twenty years, and my split-cane rod trailing behind me, I walked towards the river, my mind drifting, speculating vaguely on midges, on poppies and cornflowers, on field-mice, on the earth turning, on the choreography of swallows, on sex (a lot), on my father, on René

Magritte, on cloud formations, on whatever else came to mind or crossed my eye.

But most consistently I imagined myself as an old man in his middle seventies (I was then in my mid-forties) with slightly mad, rheumy eyes and grave marks on my hands – at seventy-four I have none, as it happens – crossing that same field.

I was usually early and would sit for a time on the bank smoking through the dusk, watching the last shreds of sunset dying, the colours around me draining away, the building opposite becoming a silhouette and the last swallow metamorphosing into the first bat, harbinger of the sea-trout's hour.

And then, usually simultaneously or almost so, a sound which is for me among the more thrilling sounds in the world – the splash of the first heavy sea-trout out there in the dark.

* * * * *

So for several years almost every night when I was at the cottage I cast for sea-trout, and lost many more than I turned. This was because I never really learnt not to strike when they took. With salmon it's the same, but far easier, because they take quietly and move off with the fly or spinner in their mouth as gently as a water spaniel retrieving a mallard, and giving you plenty of time to decide when to lift the rod. With a sewin, however, they seize the fly with a ferocious series of jerks and splashes and instinctively one tends to react at once and, as they have (or are said to have) 'soft mouths', most often they pull the fly free. Now and again, of course, I got it right, often strangely enough, more than once on the same night, but on the whole not. Even so it was always thrilling because, unlike brownies who can sulk not just for one evening but, if the conditions aren't just so, for a week or even longer, sewin will almost inevitably rise to the fly with dramatic panache several times in an evening, so there is always that thrill even if you eventually return home empty-handed. Better of course if you have been lucky. It was a deep satisfaction to me to speed through the black night at thirty miles an hour with a brace of fat silver sewin in my basket, as deep a satisfaction as any other in my life.

There was, however, a hazard both going to or coming back from the water, if I wished to try a particular pool. To reach it you had to leave the main road at its highest point and take a lane down to the river. At a certain turning you passed a farmyard. In it lurked two dogs, a Welsh collie and an alsatian. They would wait until I was actually passing the entrance and then hurl themselves at my scooter, growling and barking, eyes rolling and teeth bared. I believe in retrospect it was, for the dogs, a mixture of fun and a territorial warning. They never actually bit me or tried to unseat me. They laid no ambush. They soon dropped away and returned to the farmyard. After a time I got to quite enjoy their predictable aggression. It provided a renewable rush of adrenalin, especially on my return in the dark.

Sea-trout fishing in itself is, if unaccompanied, at times

quite a creepy activity. Shakespeare's Macbeth speaks of the west yet glimmering with some streaks of day, of good things of day beginning to droop and drown, of night's black agents getting their act together, and yet it is exactly that moment that the sewin-fisherman is waiting for. The landscape changes radically. Space seems to contract or expand. Trees and bushes assume different and less reassuring shapes. Above all and most alarming, when crossing a field, the ground appears to rear up. It's only a cow, of course, but none the less startling for that. Not at all superstitious, I quite enjoy this Blair witch aspect of night fishing, but I did have one quite genuinely unnerving experience.

*　　*　　*　　*

I have no horror of bats. Not wearing my hair up like an Edwardian debutante, I have no fear of tonsorial invasion, and besides it was most probably a myth even at the time. When I fished exclusively for sewin I welcomed the bats' appearance as a fanfare to the evening's work. I am unfazed by their banking and turning close to my face. I can, if necessary, handle one. Quite recently one got into the house and the family caught it in an old fishing-net where it became hopelessly entangled and they became hysterical. On my return I was able to liberate one wing and claw and then the other and eventually release it, enjoying of course the family's repelled awe.

Still, and despite having 'adopted' in Chester zoo (at their request) a fruit bat, I don't really like them. I'm not turned on by their fetishistic combination of fur and leather-like wing. I dislike the way they hibernate and sleep in huge colonies like left-luggage offices full of badly rolled umbrellas, but above all I don't like their mean, vicious little faces resembling tiny East End gangsters wearing stocking masks. I'm not in awe of them, however, but once, one of them gave me a nasty fright, a bad turn.

*   *   *   *

Like many night-anglers I have had my fly taken by a bat in flight. It is a somewhat Surrealist experience having to play it, to tire it and then reel it in down from the air instead of up from under the water, but it works all right and after a few minutes it was in the net, held, unhooked and released. My other bat incident was more unusual, more grotesque.

I was casting away one evening when suddenly my rod kicked, but it wasn't a fish, it didn't even feel like a fish and, having checked the fly, I carried on casting. Almost at once I began to hear an unidentifiable noise out on the water. It sounded like someone dragging a small sack full of wet entrails through a bog. It seemed to be getting louder, so I reeled in, got a torch out of my fishing bag, and turned it on. It wasn't hard to locate the source of this strange noise, but harder to identify what it was: gleaming and malevolent eyes and an almost shapeless body, part-floating, part-submerged, doggy-paddling erratically towards me. It was, I realised eventually, a bat, *the* bat I'd knocked with my rod, bringing it down into the water. Bats, it seems, are not strong swimmers. It floundered slowly through the shallows and, in a series of floppy jerks, on to the pebbles. I imagined it would dry off and fly off, but it did not. I realised I could have injured it, but couldn't think what I could do about it, so I left it there, walked the short distance to the neck of the next pool, and began to fish again. Several minutes later I heard something to my left, glanced down and there, only a few feet away, was the near-formless bedraggled bat, crepitating towards me. There was something about it which reminded me of the malevolent creatures in the ghost stories of M. R. James. Even for an atheist it was disturbing.

So I moved several pools away and began to fish again. Half an hour later, this time illuminated by a quarter-moon which had emerged from behind the clouds, I watched with mounting panic the thing flopping and crawling on target – me.

So I fled.

*   *   *   *

Months later I met an eminent zoologist at a party and told him this tale. His explanation was that I had probably disoriented the poor creature's radar when it collided with my rod-tip and was knocked into the water. In consequence it had become fixed on my rod and, given that I was the other end, me. I wasn't totally convinced by this explanation and neither, judging by the certainty with which he proposed it, was he. Still at least it makes some kind of sense.

As for me, I evolved a fantasy. Years later in London I go down to the front door in my kaftan to bring in the milk. Bending down to pick up the bottles I find myself eye to eye with the bat, very much the worse for wear, on the top step. It is eyeing my exposed throat, bracing itself with all its remaining strength, for a final, vengeful leap.

*   *   *   *   *

So from May, when the first run of large sewin happens, through June – the best month, July – variable, August – the worst month, and September – improving again, I fished the Teifi every night I could, but quite often it wasn't on. Old people are given to the belief that when they were young it was always summer. Anglers too: warm, a light breeze, overcast. In reality it often rains and, in West Wales, a lot. Fishermen are natural masochists and find a certain pleasure in crawling home like drowned rats and an added justification for glugging down whisky in the lighted inn.

What can stop you, especially in a spate river, is if the water has risen to flood level and is fast and powerful enough to uproot trees and create powerful and dangerous currents. The Teifi in itself was not, within my experience, a violent river. It was, however, particularly prone to the other effect of a spate – the radical discoloration of the water. It rose, I was told, amongst bogs, and after heavy or sustained rain, overflowed into them, absorbing vast quantities of highly concentrated mud. Overnight it became the colour of naval cocoa, and unlike some rivers took a surprisingly long time to clear. There were two ways to overcome this obstacle if you were determined to fish on. The first was to set up a spinning rod (shorter and with bigger rings) and a fixed-spool reel; a comparatively new device about which my father was rather dismissive, as we took our tea and watched a young man using one in the garden of a river-fringed hotel in the North of England the year before he died.

There is no question, however, that it makes spinning easier. The fixed reel, lightweight and elegant, does most of the work for you . . . (If well aware of the advantages and mechanism of the fixed reel or, alternatively, entirely indifferent to them, perhaps you should jump this paragraph and the two which follow it.) You push a slender sprung metal bar across the front of the spool to release it, but keeping a thumb on the line to stop letting it run free until, with a mere flick of the wrist, you send the lure shooting effortlessly across the water and, when it's where you want it, a turn of the handle and the constraining metal bar shoots back across the spool and the lure plops into the water ready to wind in.

What's more, if a fish takes (in Britain most likely salmon, sewin, pike or perch, in tropical waters, using a massive version of the fixed reel, the great marlin or leaping sailfish) you just carry on winding in. This works because the reel is so geared that the fish is always under pressure and yet can still strip off line – there is a knob on the front to adjust how *much* pressure, dependent on the size and fighting capacity of the fish in question.

I am no engineer and am totally inadequate at describing any piece of mechanism. I thought I'd better try it here, though, for the benefit of those who have no conception of the fixed reel and wanted at least an idea of it. I would also say this: examined in reality they are immediately understood and, following a few minutes of instruction, almost absurdly easy to use. (Readers who took my advice for the reasons given can, if they choose, start again from here.)

My father's objection, and I absolutely sympathise with it, was not that the fixed reel makes casting so much easier – as a comparatively lazy man he would have come to terms with that – but that, once into a fish, the angler has no need to use his or her judgement as to how to play it, when to let it run, when to hold it, when to reel it in. The fixed reel does all that for you.

Even so, when the Teifi was inky black I would sometimes spin for sewin in the afternoon and occasionally with success. Once we went to the river *en famille* for a picnic and Paddy hooked a good fish on a spoon, only to lose it at the net. It was, although naturally I didn't know it, the last time we fished together.

*   *   *   *   *

There was also a small tributary of the Teifi which, by not flooding into bogs, cleared much earlier. It was, however, very overhung by trees, and there was really only one pool worth fishing and to do that only a couple of yards where you could stand and cast without either catching a tree behind you or large bushes in front of you. It was, however, at dusk and beyond, a-splash with sewin. Sometimes I'd hook one, once I caught one, but there were a great many underwater hazards and of course, in the encroaching dark, it was easy to finish up high in a tree and, in attempting to dislodge the fly, spooking every fish in the pool. Still it was somewhere to go and rather 'secret' (I can't remember who put me on to it) in that you had to cross a farmyard to get to it.

* * * * *

At some point during the Gaer years we got to know a family, none of whom fished, but whose fairly large house included in its freehold quite a long beat of the Teifi which they said I could use whenever I wanted. I added it, therefore, to the rest of the pools available.

The family were the Empsons: William, the famous poet and essayist, his dashing South African wife, stylishly dressed in the sado-masochistic mode, and hippyish young people ad lib, some of whom were their children, or perhaps stepchildren.

It was a truly Bohemian set-up in the Augustus John tradition. There was for a start very little furniture; the ageing poet, his fine head partially framed by a long white beard growing from *under* his chin, sat in an otherwise empty room in a deck-chair

113

reading, with calm concentration, a copy of *The Times*. The kitchen, however, presided over by his glamorous and lively chatelaine, was as restless and noisy as a troop of the bandalog. When it was time to eat, Empson carefully folding up his *Times*, we sat at a huge table on long benches (although our host and hostess had proper chairs at each end). As it was getting dark, one of the youngsters was dispatched to bring back a light bulb – they were apparently at a premium in the house – and, once it was plugged in, Madam served us huge helpings of pig from a great cauldron suspended over a burning tree. She told Diana they'd bought a whole dismembered pig from a farmer, head and all (probably slaughtered illegally) and bunged the lot into the cauldron with a daily boost of vegetables. It was, while one couldn't help but wonder what part of the pig's anatomy had landed up on one's plate, delicious. Afterwards there was the rolling up and smoking of what *Private Eye* then called 'exotic cheroots', although I can't remember W.E. indulging. Indeed he was almost silent throughout the evening, but just now and again he would make an enigmatic if seerlike announcement, e.g. 'In Mandarin Chinese the word for "Alas" is the same as the word for "Hurrah"'.

It was a memorable evening but not to be repeated, as, very soon, although they hadn't been there long, they sold the house by auction. This was perhaps a wise move, as it was clear that Mrs E was a stranger to brooms, brushes, cloths, mops, soap and especially a flush brush.

I went to the auction, held in a room above a pub, out of pure nosiness. William sat by himself, his wife and the rest of the household in a group. That afternoon I listened, for the first time, fascinated as a rabbit watching a weasel dancing, to a Welsh auctioneer. I didn't realise then, of course, that a decade later, my own fortunes would hang on the expert mixture of the *faux-naif* and low cunning.

'People may wonder why the *distinguished* poet who but recently added distinction to our little community by living amongst us should, so comparatively soon after its purchase, have decided to sell his substantial house . . .'

(I rather wondered this myself: no more pig in the pot? Had the last electric light-bulb failed?)

'The reason', the auctioneer continued, 'is that Mr Empson has been summoned by the Government to occupy an important advisory post involving being called to Number 10, Downing Street at a moment's notice. Therefore . . .' etc. etc.

I looked at Empson during this absurd rigmarole. He remained totally impassive. Indeed, I've often wondered if he hadn't fed the auctioneer the whole story.

So the Empsons went and later I discovered that the bit of river I'd been fishing believing it to be theirs was the wrong stretch. I thought of it then, and I continued to use it, knowing that it was unlikely that anyone would object, as 'The False Empson Beat'. It was, by the way, on the 'False Empson Beat' that I winged the bat.

There were salmon in the Teifi, but I never tried to catch

one on purpose, nor, as might have happened, hooked one by accident on a sewin fly or while spinning. I was somehow in awe of salmon. I'd watched Tom kill one, but felt they were beyond me. Yet I saw them all right from time to time. Some nights I even watched poachers setting snares under the opposite bank, although my old anarchist principles forbade me to report them. Furthermore they seemed aware of this and wished me a cheerful 'Good evening'. More likely, though, local poachers, many of them drawn from a single village, had a fearsome reputation, and sometimes fought pitched battles with the water bailiffs. To betray them to the authorities would have been as unhealthy as to put the finger on one of the mob who had given you a big 'Hello' in the local New York deli.

The salmon and sea-trout they caught exchanged hands no doubt at the staff entrance of local hotels. These local ne'er-do-wells bore little relation to the organised gangs who have largely replaced them today, with their vans, electroids and dynamite.

What did make me angry and disgusted in relation to the salmon of the Teifi, however, was committed in broad daylight and was not even illegal.

Several miles upriver, beyond my fishing boundaries, were the Cenarth Falls, a local beauty spot. The falls, while in no way rivalling Niagara, were quite sensational and, if we had guests, we'd sometimes drive them there. We were never alone, and the cafés, ice-cream vans and so on didn't enhance the prospect, but it was, even so, well worth a visit.

Given the right conditions the salmon would gather in the pool below the fall and then, often falling back but never giving up, would leap and leap, an awe-inspiring sight, until they gained the top and could press on to their breeding grounds. On the banks would gather men with spinning rods and big lures bristling with treble hooks which they would cast across the pool at the bottom of the falls and reel rapidly in. There was no question of a fish taking the bait, their whole preoccupation was pressing up and on, but the 'anglers' had every chance of foul-hooking one and dragging it to the shore, using the strongest possible tackle.

I see, in a more recent guide to fishing in Wales, you must have a season ticket to fish around the falls. This, as opposed to daily or weekly permits, may have helped put off the piscatorial yobs, and I hope anyway there are now local laws against this odious practice.

Once, back on my own water, I saw some boys using the same method over some small rapids. Indeed one of their number was up a tree telling his companions where and when to cast. I strode towards them to remonstrate – they were after all very small boys whereas the assassins of Cenarth Falls were largely in their twenties and given to tattoos, never a good omen when it comes to confrontation.

On reaching them, however, I discovered they were not trying to foul-hook salmon, but the odious lamprey, that they had already killed four or five and were engaged in hauling yet another. Rather than rebuke them I was more inclined to cheer. This may seem inconsistent, but the lamprey is a foul thing. Here is the dictionary definition (Concise Oxford): 'Eel-like pseudo-fish with sucker mouth, pouch gills and seven spiracles and a fistula on top of head.'

It doesn't sound, and indeed is not, attractive; it resembles one of the more repellent inventions of the Flemish topographers of Hell, but that can be forgiven. What it does, though, its *modus vivendi*, is truly abhorrent. Just as the foul-hookers wait upstream for the brave salmon, so the lampreys lurk by shallows the fish must pass and then glide forward, attach themselves to its side with their 'sucker-mouth', and then, immovably clamped in place, suck in the flesh. They are meant, once you remove a part of their innards which is poisonous, to be a delicacy, and so they should be, feeding as they do on fresh – no, living – salmon. King John, our only king with no apologist whatsoever, died of a surfeit of the organ-pipelike horrors. They were in fact made for each other.

*   *   *   *   *

And so I fished on in the Teifi until we sold the cottage and moved elsewhere. As to why, all will be told in time . . .

8

BUT I DON'T LOVE THEM

At this point, the end of the Sixties, I intend to digress from a more or less chronological approach to my life on the water to write a chapter on salmon aka salmons, as the Welsh, more logically, call them. For some salmon are the reason to fish, trout a mere substitute when conditions are wrong or geography inhospitable to the 'King of Fish'.

Neither of these reasons applies in my case. There were plenty of salmon in the Teifi and the conditions ideal for spinning – a flood beginning to subside – often applied. I could have hooked one by chance when spinning for sewin or even fly-fishing; sea-trout flies are quite large enough to irritate salmon into taking. I could have done but the fact is I didn't and, to be frank, I wasn't at all upset about it. I certainly never deliberately set out to take a salmon, but why?

Fear of failure was certainly part of it. I knew I could (sometimes) catch trout or sewin. To cast fruitlessly for salmon when I might have been grassing their less imperious cousins seemed to me unappealing. Digging a little deeper I admired, but didn't envy, the salmon's life – its years at sea, its exclusive biological urge to reach its place of origin, mate and most often die. The trout stayed put. It took our flies and lures because it was deceived, not just out of temper. It has its cosy domestic side. But what about sewin? They go to sea. While undeniable, the point is they don't go far. The sea-trout is like an adolescent who plays hooky to go to a three-day rock festival. The salmon more like a backpacker who spends several years in India. I got to think I'd never take a salmon, and then one day I received an invitation.

* * * * *

Before I met her Diana had lived a somewhat picaresque life, most of it wild, even dangerous. Some of it was intensely disheartening too, but there was a calmer, more encouraging passage. This was when the Wolheims, Anne still among her best friends, Richard a respected philosopher, took her in, virtually adopted her, and introduced her to a wide social spectrum, some connected with the Gaitskellite Labour Party, others writers, painters and sacred monsters.

Anne's sister Elizabeth was married to Christopher
Glenconner and they too became warm friends. Luckily for me
when I first met them through Diana, they took to me also, and
when Christopher discovered I shared his passion for fishing he
invited not only me, but Diana and the three kids to be his guests
at Archiestown in Scotland, so that I could fish for a salmon on the
River Spey. Naturally I accepted, perhaps in retrospect rather too
eagerly, given that later I was told what my rod alone cost, but by
chance we discovered that Rachel and Jonathan Miller had bought
a house in the village so we were able at least to prevent
Christopher from having to fork out for our hotel on top of
everything else. What I never really solved, though, was why the
Millers had bought a house there. Admittedly Jonathan had just
made a documentary about local malt whiskies but, as he neither
drinks whisky nor fishes it's not that much clearer. It was a nice,
rather austere house, but they sold it fairly soon anyway.

I've no recollection how we got there. Did we fly? Arrive by
train? We certainly didn't drive. Did we perhaps stay en route at
Glen, Christopher's country seat in the Lowlands? I stayed there
once and fished from a boat on a small, presumably stocked, lake
where I caught some quite large trout while one of Christopher's
daughters, then about fifteen, stood smiling mysteriously in the
reeds like Miss Jessop in *The Turn of the Screw*.

*   *   *   *   *

The Highlands and the first morning found me, Christopher and our fellow anglers (somewhat choleric old gentlemen in meticulously shabby tweeds whom I came to think of as 'the hanging judges') and in addition a very young man I gathered to be a guards' officer.

First we drew lots as to which beat would be ours that day and then, outside the hotel, were introduced to our gillies. "How posh," I thought.

Mine was so perfect in every detail it was as if Central Casting had sent him along for an Ealing Comedy. In his sixties, squat and sturdy, ginger hair sprouting from every visible orifice, he was called Angus. He also made it clear that he was the reverse of pleased to have drawn me. For a start I was wearing thigh-waders whereas everyone else had on breast-waders. This provoked him, as we walked down to the river, to evoke a figure who was, for him, the measure of everything – 'the auld Laird'. I presumed this paragon to have been the hereditary riparian before it was sold, whether by profligate heirs or of necessity, and let out to parties of Sassenachs or Yanks, of necessity rich and, in the case of the former, distinguished members of the Establishment. I was obviously neither.

We reached the wide river and got into a boat.

'Aye the auld Laird would no allow a boat,' he told me; a shameful betrayal necessitated by my wretched thigh waders. 'He used to say, "If you canna wade, you canna fish".'

My rods, both for fly or spinner, passed muster because Christopher had lent me them (I wouldn't have trusted my

122

father's, unused for thirty years, and I'd no spinning rod or reel.)
The auld Laird hadn't much approved of spinning anyway, I
gathered. Nevertheless that was what we were going to do – spin
from a boat. Even in these degenerate times I gathered, spinning
was only tolerated when the water was over a certain depth. Angus
had, to this end, looked at a post sticking out of the water like a
large ruler, but with one bolder white mark to indicate which
method was either obligatory or permissible. That morning the
water was just over the spinning mark, there had been heavy rain
the previous week, but, by the amount of the board still damp
above it, it was obviously going down fast. Even so, Angus decided
we'd spin – I suspect he doubted I could cast at all, but any fool
could master the fixed spool reel. He was, however, rather puzzled
by my rods in general, all from Hardy's and well cared for, and
indeed how I could afford to be of the company at all.

'Did you pay for yoursel tae fush here?' he asked me. 'No,'
I said, as neutrally as I could, for I refused to rise to such a clumsy
fly. 'I'm a guest of Lord Glenconner.' But if I thought that would
put him in his place I'd underestimated him.

'Aye,' he said, 'that's what I reckoned.'

He told me I could start fishing and where to cast. He was
clearly surprised, although naturally he said nothing, to realise I'd
done it before. He was still curious, though, unable to place me;
not an old-style gent but not *nouveau riche* either. He asked me
what I did for a living – he'd probably got me down as a rat-
catcher. I told him I was a journalist.

Earlier on he'd taken in Diana and the kids who'd come to wish me luck. She would have looked dressed to perfection in the King's Road, but a little out of place in the land of the Barbour jacket. The kids were very Sixties, with long tangled hair, jeans and torn old sweaters. I had an old vaguely waterproof garment more suitable indeed for rat-catching than fishing for salmon, cords and a far too jaunty hat. Angus probably thought we were on the breadline; me scribbling in an attic to keep the wolf from the door, the kids playing with a dead cat in the airless court below.

'It'll be good for the bairns tae get some fresh air in their lungs, and your wee wifie an a',' he said, not unkindly.

I asked him if he'd ever been to London. Once, he told me, but predictably hadn't liked it. It was 'a' petrol fumes and black faces.'

Nothing before lunch, a substantial spread (game pie and the like) and several malts, no doubt those recorded by Jonathan. Neither the hanging judges nor the young soldier had touched anything. We returned to our gillies.

It was around two p.m. About an hour and a half later the line stopped dead in mid-stream as though I'd hooked something on the bottom. Angus mimed both silence and complete lack of movement. The line began to run gently off the fixed reel. Angus shouted at me to raise my rod quite hard. I did so, and all hell broke loose. Angus rowed towards a pebble beach so I could play it from the shore. He pulled the boat up further along and joined me with a net. I was into my first salmon.

* * * * *

And of course it was very thrilling, but not as thrilling as all that. Being on a spinner all I had to do was keep my rod tip up and wind in, and at last, for he didn't give in easily, he tired and I beached him over the pebbles. This, a method I'd learnt when landing sea-trout, modified Angus's low opinion of my potential, but perhaps not as much as the fiver I gave him. From then on he mellowed as far as was within his nature and 'the Auld Laird' lay quiet in his grave. The salmon weighed about eight pounds. Nor was Angus displeased when he heard later that none of the hanging judges had touched anything, although the subaltern, like me, had killed one of about the same size.

Before I returned for supper chez Miller, the anglers all met up in the hotel bar to punish Jonathan's malts and discuss the day. The subaltern and I were congratulated none too enthusiastically except by Christopher, and then one of the HJs asked me what fly I'd used. In naïve good faith I told them I hadn't used a fly. I'd been spinning. The effect of this admission transformed the bar into an H. M. Bateman cartoon. Its title would have been: 'The man who boasted of catching a salmon on a spinner when the water was at fly-level only.' But it was above the spinning level, I told them (little did I imagine that morning I'd be defending the ginger ogre). It was just above the mark on the post. Well, it may have been, they conceded, but my gilly knew perfectly well it was going down rapidly. Next day, however, unless it rained heavily in the night

125

(one of them tapped the hotel barometer which was set on fair) it was fly only. 'Not my fault'. 'Novice', and so on. As a peace offering one of them offered me another rare and intoxicating malt and I realised that, on reflection, I had caught my fish after all on a spinner. They had failed on a fly.

While sharing a pee, the subaltern admitted that his gilly, too, had allowed him to spin, only luckily none of the HJs had thought to ask him (an officer and a gentleman after all) what fly he'd used. As for Christopher, he seemed to have been rather tickled by this storm in a hip-flask.

*　*　*　*　*

I'd thought quite a lot during the day on the tradition of the licensed rudeness of the Scottish gilly; a concept dating back to John Brown at least and perhaps long before that.

I tried on many theories, but decided the most likely was the Scottish nannies favoured by the British aristocracy. The bluntness of the gilly was as reassuring a return to the nursery as a plateful of spotted dick with custard.

*　*　*　*　*

Next morning Angus was affability itself. I expect someone, Christopher perhaps, had told him that I'd saved him from the gallows.

So I used the fly, a 'Hairy Mary', as far as I can recall. (I'd brought up Tom's case, full of large, multi-coloured beauties, but Angus had dismissed them as 'Irish', although another time he claimed that, if fish were on the take, you could tie on a 'liquorice allsort and expect success'.)

Our beat that day didn't need the boat and was shallow enough along the shore to allow me to use the despised thigh-waders, although it got much deeper some distance out, but near enough to cover. Angus's only criticism was that I was casting too straight in front of me before the current carried the fly round, the normal practice when wet fly-fishing for trout. He wanted a more oblique angle. 'Forget the troot!' he barked every time I reverted. 'Forget the troot!'

And then again the line stopped before moving steadily upstream stripping line off the reel. 'Noo!' shouted Angus and I lifted the rod tip and struck. This time it was much more exciting because one was much more in contact with the fish, instead of just winding in whatever. You have to judge when to let it run, when to hold it, to 'honour' it by lowering your rod when it leaps, to run after it up or down the bank. It took about twenty minutes; a fresh-run fish with the sea-lice on it. It weighed about two pounds more than the one caught on the spinner.

Angus congratulated me warmly and this time was rewarded with a tenner. Naturally he was eager for me to cast again immediately. 'He may have a chum with him,' he suggested optimistically. He didn't, but later, just to rub salt in the wounds of the HJs, I took quite a large sea-trout. They'd caught nothing. Neither had Christopher, but I gather he hadn't cared too much for them and seemed to twinkle at their discomfiture. Next day we went back to London and, thanks to the deep-freeze, formed the impressive centrepiece of a cold buffet at a party we gave to celebrate the publication of my first book.

* * * * *

This, you might suppose, was the moment when I became a convert to salmon, but I didn't. Why? It's a difficult one to answer. It's a more expensive activity if you insist on the great Scottish rivers, but in my case there were salmon in both the Teifi when I fished it and the Usk which replaced it. Indeed the Usk in recent years has had a considerable (and improving) autumn run, yet in twenty years I only caught two, both on a spinner. More shaming, in both cases I was with another angler keen to have a go in perfect conditions (a flood beginning to ebb) and thereby throwing down a glove.

The first was Ricky Fatah, the laid-back Californian composer and rock drummer who, only a year or two previously, had mastered trout fishing with awe-inspiring ease on this very water. Of course he landed a salmon whereas I, equally pre-dictably, lost one, and although he left next day, impelled me to continue until the score was even. Then I returned to trout.

My other 'rival' is the play- and script-writer, Julian

Mitchell, a dear friend who has a Welsh house some way down the river from us. Out fishing with him I caught a salmon on a spinner, but he lost one *on a fly*, an incident he somehow managed to turn into a moral victory, but then in every department we are as competitive as Siamese fighting-fish. He, however, is almost exclusively interested in catching salmon on the fly and I must admit is very successful at it. Whenever we meet during the season he tells me how many he's had. He transmits this enviable information in a very casual tone of voice which only just conceals a Peter Pan-like crow of triumph. It's as well he's not much interested in trout and quite clumsy in pursuit of them. This has saved us from too many temptations to score off each other.

He is, however, not only lovable but extremely generous. A few winters ago a lorry drew up on the banks of the Usk and the two men released two hundred half-pound brown trout (fish-farm-bred naturally, but of local origin). They were, it happens, a spontaneous gift from Julian.

Neither he nor I were to know, as we watched the trout enthusiastically breaking the surface in the late autumn sun, that twelve months later, for practical reasons, we would decide to sell the beautiful house with its mile of fishing and move to Berkshire.

Incidentally, I happen to have heard that Julian has written my obituary for a national newspaper. I can't believe he won't say something bitchy about my fishing.

*   *   *   *   *

My fishing for trout doesn't rule out salmon fishing provided I'm invited. Quite soon, for example, the BBC are flying me out to Nova Scotia to try to catch salmon for a travel programme. I've read somewhere that it's so easy to catch salmon in Nova Scotia it can become quite tedious, if it weren't for having to watch out for grizzly bears, one's piscatorial rivals, putting on fat for their winter hibernation.

Once before I was paid to fish for salmon. With my son Tom as my minder, the *Evening Standard* flew me out to Arctic Russia on the eve of my sixty-ninth birthday. I remember the scene as I arrived. A hundred yards away lay the camp, its tents of various shapes and sizes silhouetted against a dramatic evening sky. Below it the great Jokenga river rolled between boulders and outcrops of rock, and beyond was a long hill in whose shelter a larch wood had grown up.

Yet it wasn't so much the landscape that intoxicated us, but the sense of a vast wilderness, the departing helicopter the only link with elsewhere, the nearest settlement 80 miles away. What's more, this sense of wonder never left us. It's what I've found most difficult to get across to perplexed friends. How could I, hedonistic and overweight, enjoy fishing for salmon at the end of the season in the Russian Arctic Circle?

Dave Wilkinson, the Geordie proprietor of Flying Ghillies, British agent for Norway's 'Arctic Wild Adventures', was in no danger of being done under the Trades Description Act. He'd promised me Spartan amenities, mosquitoes and uncertain weather, and he fulfilled these promises to the letter. The four-day gale was in cahoots with the torrential rain; the former blowing the tent flaps open, however securely tied, to allow the latter to flood the floor and soak everything else. To go out for a pee in the spiky grey tundra was a nightmare, to crouch for a crap worse, but the lavatory, fifty yards away, was unspeakably dreadful. Yet I wouldn't have missed it for a week at the Gritti Palace.

The layout of the camp was simple. The largest tent housed the dining-room with its long table and, behind a curtain, the galley. Despite two small windows, it was as dark as an over-varnished 19th century oil painting, although sometimes, with much juddering, a generator managed to produce enough power to light up, intermittently, two small bulbs. Due, however, to the cooking it was always warm and cosy in the dining tent.

The chef, Anatoly, a Russian, was a plump little man who emerged from behind his curtain crying 'Good! Good!! Very good!!!' as he brought in each successive course. He was desperate to please and very upset if anything wasn't finished.

Actually the food was not at all bad. In particular the soup, especially the salmon soup; and there was always delicious thinly sliced, slightly sour black bread and good strong coffee. Drink, including spirits, you took from a cupboard and wrote down.

*   *   *   *   *

On my sixty-ninth birthday Anatoly made me an elaborate cake ringed by cloudberries. Near the dining tent was the lavoo, the Lapp version of a wigwam with a hole in the top which is supposed to let out the smoke from the blazing wood-fire beneath. Here, most evenings after dinner, we sat around on white fur rugs thrown over logs, circulating a bottle, most often vodka. Here too we got to know the Norwegians, the majority of the camp's visitors. Burly, cheerful, bearded men with pink cheeks and twinkling blue eyes, they looked to me like an outing of Father Christmases, and I amused myself deciding who worked for which store.

It was the 'Harrods Santa', in real life the editor of the Norwegian equivalent of *The Times*, who was not only extremely informative about Lapp culture, but sang beautiful and melancholy Northern folk songs in a pure true tenor.

We slept two to a tent. They were very basic: a hard-wood floor, a stove (supplemented by an oil heater in really bad weather), two iron bedsteads with narrow nylon sleeping bags, and a length of cord to hang your clothes on. No light, but then at that latitude in August there is no night, only dusk. It was theoretically possible to keep clean. There was a row of plastic buckets near the dining tent and at some distance from the camp proper a sauna, only intermittently lit, with an adjoining shower room, both primitive and rather inefficient.

Tom and I soon reverted to a state approximating to New Age travellers. In this we were abetted by Dave Wilkinson who claimed that washing destroyed the build-up of insect repellent (although I suspected the mosquitoes relished it) and that it was advisable to grow beards as well. I finished up looking like an alcoholic tramp hanging round a railway terminus, but what was odd was that we didn't get at all smelly. The purity of the air, perhaps?

Dotted around the camp stood wooden structures like hitching posts outside Western saloons. Against these rested the great two-handed salmon rods.

Dave's clients, apart from Tom and myself, were David Frusher, Jeremy Searle and Thomas Staub. David, a successful manufacturer of piano stools in Banbury, was neatly bearded with a commanding profile, and turned out with all the elegance of a late-Victorian sportsman.

David had killed many Scottish salmon, some when the weather was too bad for stalking. Jeremy, whose ex-colonial childhood is no doubt a help as an exporter of steel and chemicals largely to Africa, was, like myself, a keen trout fisherman but had never hooked a salmon. Thomas was a lanky, pipe-smoking Swiss delicatessen owner who has probably grassed more than the rest of us added together, and then there was Dave himself.

* * * * *

Despite my initial resistance to his ritual display of Geordie chauvinism, I became very fond of him. He revealed a love and understanding of nature and was a patient instructor in the wielding of a salmon. The only trouble was that my back wasn't up to it, so I reverted to my wife's birthday present, a beautiful little four-piece Farlow trout rod on which I hooked and grassed a five-pound grilse.

Strongly believing it to be too small, I returned it to the water (we were allowed to kill one fish each to take home as gravlax). David was less lucky. He hadn't taken aboard the cock-fish-only rule, and returned triumphantly to camp with a 16-pound hen. In the midst of our congratulations the Russian fishing inspector materialised, an elderly gentleman until then amiable, and he gave David a terrible roasting and confiscated the fish for the kitchen (a salmon pizza turned up next day – not one of Anatoly's happiest contributions).

Still, David grassed eight fish in all, Jeremy two, and the master, Thomas, 13. I only caught the one but partly because on the third day a gale broke and raged for 48 hours and, apart from meal-times and the boozing sessions in the lavoo, I stayed in my sleeping bag reading Mervyn Peake.

*   *   *   *

I'm not alone in my preference for trout. An Edwardian angler and author I am unable to track down actually referred to salmon as 'that great oily fellow', a denigrating description that cannot have endeared him to those of his contemporaries who fished the chalk streams of the south during May and June only to head north to intercept the anadromous roe and milt missiles on their obsessive and frequently fatal journey.

One thing is certain. If it had been a salmon I'd hooked over twenty years ago on the Usk, in no way would I have hacked my way through the chest-high weeds on that narrow island to find a clearing and a sacrificial tree-stump. I respect and admire salmon, I get a thrill when I hook and land one, but I don't love them.

9

ALL CHANGE

There'll be some changes made today
There'll be some changes made'

Old Jazz Standard

Unfreeze the frame. Again I putt-putt through the Pembroke-shire night. The Sixties are raving on. In Gloucester Crescent NW1 the Surrealist masterpieces hang in the dark. The kids seem well. There are however, a few straws in the wind to suggest that Diana is beginning to feel some mild but growing discontent.

One morning, driving back from shopping in Cardigan I said something about loving our life here. Irritated, she pulled into a lay-by and told me that on the contrary she was becoming quite restless, that she loved travel and the sun (hardly a guaranteed visitor to West Wales) and would like now and again to go abroad.

At first, with my tunnel vision, I was both hurt and

perplexed. Then I realised that, without a passion for fishing, with only the kids to keep her occupied and the usual domestic chores, the cottage offered a limited prospect, year in year out. I agreed in response (if agreed isn't too positive a word in relation to Diana's wishes) to break the routine and, as long as I got *some* fishing in, to go abroad every now and again.

*   *   *   *   *

As it happened, that very next year I'd just made some money writing a film-script and, right on cue, our friends Andy and Polly Garnett asked us to stay at a farmhouse they'd bought in Tuscany (a less clichéd choice then than it was to become later) and that after a few days there, we'd drive to Venice and meet up with Tom and Candy. It all sounded a long way from Pen-y-Bryn, and so it proved.

After Venice we thanked the Garnetts and flew on to Yugoslavia, where Diana, true to her word, had booked us into a small very dull town and a pretentious but inefficient tourist hotel which nevertheless claimed to arrange fishing. There was a diet of meatballs, a rock group offering Beatle songs learnt phonetically from the records, including the Liverpool accents, and a lavatory *en suite* which, if you sat on it head-on, you burnt your thigh on the radiator, but there was indeed fishing – of a sort.

It took place on a swampy area and performed by a large number of men in caps. Their method was to cast out lines with, every few inches, red floats like miniature ping-pong balls with tiny

137

hooks suspended from them baited with luncheon meat. After a few moments the ping-pong balls began to bob about and, when hauled in, almost every hook had been taken by a very small fish which the men stripped off into buckets as if they were shelling peas. I'd no idea what these fish were, but they took my fly on almost each cast and to start with I threw them back; but the men, besides finding my rod and technique absurd, were appalled to see me let them go. To dissuade me they pointed into their open mouths and then rubbed their stomachs to show how good they were. So I gave the man next to me any I caught from then on, and he was mystified but pleased.

Suddenly I was into quite a big fish. It pulled out a lot of line but got off without breaking either my leader or my fly. Later I thought it might have been a pike or another predator grabbing the little fish on my hook. I looked up to see if any of the men in caps could mime an explanation, only to find them all gone. The reason was soon evident. The swamp was flooding, the tide presumably, and was soon over my waders, one of the most dispiriting moments for any fisherman. There was a strong current too, but I struggled through it and squelched back to the hotel. The kids enjoyed themselves in Yugoslavia, there were plenty of local children to play with (it's as well we cannot read the future) and the little girls were especially taken with Candy who, they maintained, bore a strong resemblance to the Italian film star Claudia Cardinale. For Diana and me, however, despite our proximity to the beautiful but equally unsophisticated town of

Dubrovnik, it was an anti-climax. I had to admit I'd much preferred the Giottos, the Florentine buildings, S. Marco and a meeting with that old cathedral, Peggy Guggenheim, surrounded by modern masterpieces in her truncated palazzo.

Having so enjoyed our first trip abroad and knowing the final fortnight was to be spent in Wales, I was quite looking forward to our next expedition: an invitation to stay at a villa in the south of France near St Tropez. I was wrong to look forward to it.

During the course of this book I have sometimes seen fit to deviate now and then from patrolling the river-bank, but what happened in the south of France that disastrous summer was a personal crisis and in this context irrelevant. Yet while leaving out the how and why, I think it is necessary to explain the end result. It changed a lot.

In France, orchestrated by the dry creaking of the cicadas and after almost eight years, our obsessional love died on us, not gradually, but like a light-bulb blowing, a literal illustration of those matter-of-fact but heartbreaking words of Billie Holiday:

Love is like a faucet, it turns off and on
Just when you think it's on, someone's turned it off and gone.

We returned to Wales in disorder, Di with a badly cut foot, me with a suppurating cold-sore – outward and visible signs of an inward and spiritual change. Di's reaction was to join, actually rather late in the day, the Sixties. Mine, after a typically and as always

139

surprisingly short time of readjustment, was to stagger back into the Fifties – the raver of yesteryear. I was usually drunk, as promiscuous as a rhesus monkey, tending when half-asleep to pee in the corner of rooms or a handy drawerful of cashmere sweaters – Falstaff's minion again.

Quite quickly Diana and I devised a rather detached *modus vivendi* for these two strangers who shared our names, and became reasonably friendly. One thing was certain, though, the cottage had to go. Gaer was too small. We'd led a different kind of life there. Once we'd moved Tom and Candy took to referring to it as 'the other Wales', and so it was.

*   *   *   *   *

However difficult our life at any given time, Diana has always made it a priority to find me somewhere to fish. With the cottage gone she asked me to describe my ideal. I told her it would be a Regency Gothic rectory with a serious chalk stream at the bottom of a gently sloping velvet lawn.

She started looking at once, and told me she had fallen in love with a house in Wales, and arranged for me to travel by train to Newport, Monmouthshire, where I would be met by one Major Harpur, manager of the estate on which the building stood.

'Fishing's available,' Diana had assured me.

*   *   *   *   *

140

Major Harpur turned out to be a quiet man of great charm. In the car he refused to be drawn, I suspect at Diana's insistence, as to what I might expect to see.

We drove through hilly country with mountains in the background. I got to know this route very well over the next twenty years or so, and indeed, once we'd joined the A40 I recognised various aspects and landmarks I'd taken in on the way to 'the other Wales'. It was a crisp, clear autumn day.

At last we turned off down a narrow pot-holed lane, past some old farm-buildings incorporating a barn and shippen, and there, beyond a gate, loomed the Tower, the antithesis of a Regency Gothic rectory.

The Tower was a formidably sturdy square fourteenth-century stone building designed, possibly as part of a moated wooden castle, to repel the Welsh. It might perhaps have looked a bit too like the setting for one of those electronic 'medieval' games if it were not for the fact that, in the seventeenth century, someone had knocked down the castellations, added a roof and knocked through (I imagine with some difficulty) a number of haphazardly placed windows. It was built on a mound to defy the winter floods, and surrounded by an acre or so of brambles formidable enough to drive back the Prince who'd come to rescue the Sleeping Beauty. Despite the low asking price, it would cost a fortune to put right – no water, gas or electricity for a start – but it was not to be denied. It felt both welcoming and protective, absurd I know, the pathetic fallacy at its worst. It was simply an old building and yet . . .

Diana had already said we'd have it, rather to the Major's surprise, for although liberal-minded he would probably have expected her to say, 'Providing of course that my husband agrees.' I immediately concurred.

He took me across a big field to look at the river. I could hire, he told me, over a mile of it by the year for a reasonable amount. Reaching the water and on cue, a large trout rose to take a fly, and then another. We bought the Tower and we managed. We kept it for over twenty years.

10

FLOWING
WATERS AND
EMPTY WALLS

Buying the Tower was one thing. Renovating it another. Our first architect drew very prettily but seemed unable to engage with those bureaucrats who are programmed to deny planning permission. This was, it must be admitted, especially difficult in that the Tower was a Listed Building (Class 2) and lavatories, a bathroom, electricity and gas were not that common in the fourteenth century or even the seventeenth. On the other hand, most of what Diana planned was to do with restoration and preservation: the removal of a flight of Victorian stairs in the hall and the opening up of a spiral staircase in the thick walls. The dismantling of a hideous brick Thirties fireplace from the ground floor (someone with some money must have owned the building at that time) and the destruction of all the hardboard partitions. Above all, if the roof wasn't removed, strengthened and replaced (original tiles of course) it would soon collapse. But this failed to speed them along.

So Diana replaced the architect with a colleague of a more pugnacious disposition and, item by item, he got his own way.

For the first year we lived in the house like squatters, for the second, when the building started, we camped on the by now bramble-free ground in front of it like gypsies. The workmen, carpenters, masons, electricians, roofers, gas and water engineers, arrived each day at dawn, marching in a line to start their noisy tasks. Under my breath I would sing the 'Heigh Ho' song from *Snow White*.

In the end it was done: whitewashed throughout, eclectic furniture and pictures which it somehow absorbed without effort or protest. A big window on the huge ground floor kitchen/living-room, looked out on to an oxbow pond visited by herons, swans and, once, a white egret. Under the rather muddy water were some (probably inedible) trout and dace, trapped by the recession of the winter floods. Naturally over the next two decades there were changes and additions: an extra shower and loo, an ingeniously designed extra bedroom, a conservatory *en suite*, but it was mostly in shape. The Tower, imposing but not intimidating, magical but beneficent. Around it, too, the acre of garden assumed various forms and functions but there were always blowsy old-fashioned roses that smelt wonderful.

People came to stay and were enchanted: it was an Eden – but a serpent was watching us with a fiercely disapproving eye. His chance was yet to come.

The great field was leased by the local farmer, a charming and beneficent old gentleman, who smiled at our picnics by the river and encouraged us to collect wood or gather mushrooms.

He had two sons and, deciding to retire, handed over the farm for them to run together. This didn't work out, so he divided the land in two. The top half, a lot of it hill and above the A40, went to one, a man as amiable as himself; the bottom half to a very different character, a tall, well-built and wiry form with red side whiskers, a cap, seemingly welded to his head, and known to the village children as 'Dai Grumpy'. It was he who had overlooked us with growing resentment at our behaviour during his father's reign and was now able to make our lives extremely difficult.

*   *   *   *   *

I was working in New York and Diana and a friend came over and we shared a borrowed 'railway apartment' with two cats. It was a tight fit. I called it 'Privacy Palace'. There was lots to do in New York, old friends to see, and Alberta Hunter to listen to, a grand old Blues singer of the Twenties, recently rediscovered and belting it out in 'The Cookery' in Greenwich Village. I could tell, though, there was something on Diana's mind. Eventually she came out with it.

'We may have to sell the Tower,' she said. 'The new farmer is really hostile. He's making it impossible!'

His main decree was to allow no one, unless they were carrying a rod (for he knew I'd rented the fishing) to cross his land and if anyone tried he would zoom down from his farmhouse up the hill (had he field glasses?) and shout at them from his four-wheeled vehicle, his face white with rage. His actual threats were on the bizarre side, 'Get off my land,' he'd yell, 'or I'll nail your ears to the ground!' But none the less terrifying for that.

Among the canyons of New York the distant ranting from a farmer in a Welsh valley seemed far away. With easy and arrogant confidence, I said I'd go and talk to him on my return. After all, I thought, I've been on telly. But there was actually nothing less likely to impress Dai Grumpy, and good on him there.

So when I got back and next visited Brecon, I set out to disarm the demon king. There had been a terrible storm in the night and part of the old barn complex, put up apparently without foundations, had collapsed. Dai Powell was looking at it with a practical eye. My opening regret at the destruction of such a fine structure was ignored.

I tried again: 'Mr Powell,' I said, 'I hear you are stopping my guests from walking in your field. They all know about shutting gates, you know.'

He came up to me then, saying that he knew that was the

real reason for my visit, and he was determined. No one from the Tower except for me with my rod was allowed on his land! Now! Never! Never!

I asked him why.

His answer was surprising. 'Because', he said fiercely, 'I disapprove of your life-style.'

I was fascinated by his use of this word 'life-style'. Did he hear it on TV? 'What do you mean 'life-style?' I asked him.

'Ten people staying and only three bedrooms!'

Where did he get that from?

'The builders!'

'In fact,' I told him, 'while there are indeed three main rooms, there are smaller ones tucked away in the walls and a caravan too (Diana had commissioned it from an imaginative craftsman – a pastiche of a gypsy wagon that somehow avoided whimsy). 'Also,' I finished what I felt to be a knock-down argument, 'many of our guests are families. Surely husbands and wives with young children can share rooms?'

There was a very short silence and then he said, 'Nobody is allowed on my land! Nobody!' He turned his back.

He kept it up for a long time.

*　*　*　*　*

The worst trick he pulled, and I think Diana was there alone, was when he came to destroy three trees in the field, trees forming a rough circle round the Tower. He set them on fire rather than cut them down and that at dusk. The effect was not unlike the fiery crosses of the Ku-Klux-Klan and Diana was, as I imagine he intended, quite frightened. None the less we, and especially her, for she was there much more than I was, stuck our heels in. We complained to Major Harpur who told him to watch it, and to his father who said no one, not even his mother, had any control over him. Still, at least he knew that others were aware. He knew his rights too. He could stop anyone he liked walking through his field, leased or no.

His father also told us something quite odd about him – he had never taken a holiday in his life – not even a day. He was in fact a 'workaholic' (a word I hate, but the only one appropriate here), and this of course explains another angry criticism he'd directed at our guests during my fruitless would-be attempt to appease him. 'Free holidays,' he sneered. 'That's what they're here for – free holidays.' One can see how, for a man who has never taken a holiday, the sight of all those relaxing and, worse still, *English* smart-arses, must have been at best irritating. It didn't help either that one evening, walking by the river with his wife, they should have seen a beautiful girl, now one of our most eminent progressive lawyers, swimming naked as a naiad.

* * * * *

During the Dai Grumpy years I, who was there less often except to fish, believed him to continue to shout and threaten. This was apparently not the case. He still roared up to guests *sometimes*, but less and less, and our guests continued to walk the field. Finally he calmed down to the extent of tipping his cap at Diana, and eventually even me, as he opened the gate adjoining the Tower at precisely 8 a.m. and 5 p.m. to inspect his domain. That 'even me' is based on something he told someone, presumably in a public house. 'Mrs Melly's all right,' he said, 'but *he's* like a bear with a sore head.'

At all events the easing of our relationship soon improved to the point where he helped her put up an electric fence to stop the sheep, his sheep admittedly, from getting into the garden at the oxbow end and some time later he came up to warn me about the bull.

*　*　*　*　*

In the spring he grazed his sheep in the big field. Later there were cattle: adult cows, bullocks, calves, heifers, and a bull. Now a bull by itself is an unknown quantity, but with a herd usually all right, although naturally you don't walk through the middle or too close. You give the bull respect and he in turn, while sometimes looking at you passing, ignores you.

It's well known, too, that some breeds are less to be trusted than others. The 'map-like' Friesian has a bad record, but famously the worst is the pretty little Guernsey with its long lashes and charming café-au-lait coat. The best-behaved bulls on the other hand are taken to be the solid Hereford, brown-red in colour, and exceptionally even-tempered, and the Charolais, a big pinky species of French origin. In our Tower years Dai Powell had first the one, then the other. I was fascinated by the genetic results. The Charolais in particular fathered a lot of calves of his own unique colour, but there were Friesians as well. Yet it was unlikely that he could have been cuckolded.

And yet that auspicious day when Dai approached me with a warning, there *was* another bull involved.

'I wouldn't go too near the old bull today,' he warned me. 'He crossed the river and had a fight with another bull and he lost, see? He's in a bad temper!'

I thanked him. I was amazed. You could have knocked me down with a heifer! From then on a verbal greeting was added to the brief touching of the cap peak.

* * * * *

Diana and I have very different views of human motivation. She thinks Dai gradually mellowed because of time alone. Slowly he became used to us. His anger evaporated.

I tend towards a belief in trauma. In this case, for instance, we heard (the country is a better source of gossip than the drawing-rooms of Belgravia) of a crisis in his own life which may well have shaken his hard-edged puritanism. Equally I think our purchase of the fishing with built-in right of way affected him. It proved I was more than a dilettante: I was there to stay. Diana thinks that's all melodramatic nonsense. Of course we could both be in part right.

She developed, however, and I came to agree with her, a sympathy for Dai's early intransigence. He was an obsessive and committed farmer, the Welsh equivalent of Amos in Stella Gibbons' *Cold Comfort Farm.* We'd come sailing in and, under licence from his father, treated the field as if it were a pleasure garden. For him it was sacred ground. We were patronisingly casual, said Diana, and she was right.

*   *   *   *   *

The old gentleman from whom, via Major Harpur, we rented our water, died and his heirs, inheriting amongst no doubt much else, six miles of double bank fishing, decided to break it down into single bank lots of approximately a mile each and put it to auction. Financially, they would be unlikely to regret it.

Local opinion was that each stretch would go for about twelve to seventeen thousand pounds. I felt this to be optimistic. Since the announcement, too many large, chauffeur-driven motor-cars had pulled up in the lane and disgorged very tall men with Trumper haircuts, armed with salmon poles and gillies to suss out the pools. Presumably they and their clones visited every lot. To spend seventeen thousand didn't look as though it would worry these gentlemen's bank manager over much.

On 27 May, Diana, our house guest Bruce Chatwin and I drove into Brecon and took our seats in an upper room of the Wellington Hotel. The Trumperish men weren't there; they had presumably either put in bids or, more likely, employed others, less posh and intimidating in appearance, to bid on their behalf. We did this too. We asked young Simon Harpur, the Major's son, then part of his firm, later a sheep farmer and on the side a brilliant photographer, to perform the same service for us.

The auctioneer, modestly dressed and the antithesis of the laid-back *grands fromages* at Christie's and Sotheby's, stood behind a table on a raised platform. He introduced himself in a stage Welsh accent and in much the same terms as the man who sold his house for Professor William Empson. Perhaps it was the same man. Brecon and Cardigan are only about seventy miles apart.

He began by saying how inadequate he was for the task. A farm? Yes. A flock of sheep? Certainly. But this *magnificent* fishing, these twelve *wonderful* lots. No, far beyond his modest powers, but he would do his poor best. He was of course brilliant. His claiming to need a swallow of water every time the bidding slowed down was beautifully timed. The way that, while drinking it he picked up the gavel, groped for it rather, with his free hand, stirred one after another of the anxious punters into raising his bid. The first lot went for around forty-five thousand pounds, and it was not the best.

Diana and I conferred. Our 'limit' of twenty thousand pounds would go nowhere. Without the fishing, the Tower would be useless to me. We had in London just enough valuable pictures left to cover it. We decided to go for broke. All the previous lots went for about the same price. Ours was the penultimate. It was also a little longer than some and with several good holding pools for salmon. Besides there were bidders who had lost out and decided to try again. It was knocked down for forty-seven thousand, five hundred pounds.

*　　*　　*　　*　　*

That night at dinner at a rather pretentious restaurant on the way to Hay-on-Wye, Bruce Chatwin raised his glass to offer a toast. 'To the Lord of the Flowing Waters,' he said.

'No, no,' I corrected him. 'The Lord of the Empty Walls!'

11

THE GYPSY
BITCH

For twenty years I fished my mile of the River Usk and, now that it is no longer mine, I shall walk and wade its banks one more time, relying on memory alone and greeting those ghosts, both living and dead, who fished the opposite bank or alongside me or greeted me from the field, either in defiance of the early Dai Grumpy or the tacit permission of the reformed David Powell.

A constant and sad revenant was my stepson, Patrick, that bright and clever, moody and difficult child who, in late adolescence, was drawn, in increasingly cynical despair, towards the black hole of hard drugs and then, in 1980, overdosed in a squat in North London.

However devious or enraged, he was always a wonderful

(and quite strict) half-brother to Tom and Candy and they were made desperate by his death, but there is no question that Diana suffered worst. Torn by guilt, sucked down into the whirlpool of depression, she was still able to operate on a daily level, but I was always aware that, under a brittle surface, guilt and pain grappled with each other and bred monsters. And then, quite recently, she began to write about Patrick both beautifully and realistically. He is re-emerging for her as a genuine person with faults and virtues – not a scapegoat.

And for me? The worst of it, beyond my sadness over Paddy, whom I had tried ineptly, no, disastrously, to help, was my discovery that I was unable to reach, still less to comfort Diana. I just wasn't there. So I took my usual way out. On the one hand Paddy was for me the smiling boy proudly displaying the eel he'd caught in 'The Other Wales'. On the other hand he was also 'the thrilling delinquent', 'the Anarchist'. I lacked the courage or the will to be either.

So I retreated into my defensive fortifications: drink, jazz, writing, the dream of The Surrealist Revolt, and above all, fishing, my rune, my mantra, my Tibetan prayer-wheel.

*   *   *   *   *

Before we start our stroll, I shall try to give you a simplified ground-plan. My mile was not in a straight line – on the contrary it was in the shape of a horseshoe. If you stood with your back to the rear of the Tower, and the great field in front of you, all the pools were roughly the same distance, a great advantage to the indolent.

Or – think of the Tower as the hub of a wheel so all you have to do to reach the pool you've chosen is to walk along the appropriate spoke.

This description is, of course, like the tube map, over-simplified, distances approximate, but they'll do.

What's more, 'The Great Field' is not the even, geometrical billiard cloth you may have envisaged from my diagrammatic approach. It has banks and dry ditches, small plantations of thistles or nettles and some beautiful trees, but also acres of good grazing.

The pools are strung like pearls on the river's thread. They are all named – 'The Home Pool', as the name suggests, marks the end of my water, 'The Pill Box Pool' its start. We could stroll either way but, as the Usk is largely a wet-fly river, we'll fish it down.

There is indeed a pill-box overlooking the river and built presumably in case the Germans came sweeping down from the mountains – unlikely, I'd have thought. It has mostly collapsed, a few fragments of red-brick wall like a partially dismantled Lego set embedded in the muddy bank.

To gain access to the pool you have to climb over or under some permanent barbed wire and a temporary electric fence, extended for some distance along to prevent the cattle fording the river into fields belonging to another farmer. When we'd first arrived I could swing my leg elegantly over both wire and fence. By the time we left I had to crawl under like the serpent in Genesis.

A steep and slippery bank with, happily, some trees and saplings to hold on to, leads you down to the pool and its fringe of pebbles. A small riffle at the top and very deep water at the bottom, but you have to wade anyway because the near bank is overhung by trees at exactly the right height to hook your fly. Ever since I started fishing, whenever I caught a fly in a tree, I remember a piece of folklore of my childhood. 'Mr Colman makes his money by the mustard people leave on their plates', and then paraphrase it as 'Mr Hardy and Mr Farlow make their money by the flies and lures lost in trees, thickets and underwater hazards'.

Once in position you could cast and wade along a trout-rich swim under the opposite bank and there were always knocks and usually a large trout on and fighting hard. At the evening rise trout, some very big, would be rising all over the pool.

Although once you reached the deep end you had to get out of the water, climb the bank and crawl back under the hazards into the field, for some years, although it was on the short side, the 'Pill-box Pool' remained my favourite. Admittedly one very dry August, always the cruellest month for trout fishermen, I tried night after night without a single hit, but I could scarcely blame the Pill Box Pool. It was there, however, that I caught my only fish of the month – a large, handsome and totally inedible chub!

I didn't even blame the Pill Box Pool for the disaster of the following March (the Usk season starts in March, unlike those posh chalk-streams like the Test who wait until May).

It was a warm early spring day. I waded in confidently at my usual point of entry only to find myself up to my neck in feezing water. The river had, as usual, altered the whole geography of the river bottom. You had to re-explore it every year, a precept I soon took to heart.

It's the Usk, you see. I loved her, I love her, I will always love her, but she is an arbitrary, irresistible gypsy bitch, handing out tantrums and kisses indiscriminately on whim.

Don't take my word for it. After we'd been there some years, Diana, if she was going abroad on holiday and I was touring Australia, or, come to that, the Lake District, would let the fishing. Here are some random entries.

12/8/85: 'Strong wind and turned cold. No offers. M. Gould.' But he caught two trout the next evening and five the evening after that, all of them over a pound.

A week later an anonymous party booked in (although they let slip that one of them was called Toby), and between their arrival on 22 August and their departure on 2 September ('Do hurry up, Toby. The car's loaded.') they killed six salmon and returned three large trout. All this, you'll notice, took place in August, but in another rainless year of leprous algae, I was again fishless. Then on the last day I hooked something really heavy. I never caught a glimpse of it. It fought so long a small crowd gathered on the opposite bank. Finally I got it to the net. It was a huge, foul-hooked eel.

*   *   *   *   *

The distance between the Pill Box Pool and the Woodland Pool always seemed longer than it was. This is because intermittently through the trees you can see the water to your right, but you know you can't fish it – too deep to wade, the banks too sheer, and then suddenly a wood confronts you, rears up from the water's edge and turns the corner. What's more, behind the expected wire and fence is what would seem to be an impenetrable army of shoulder-high vegetation.

In fact it's not that bad. There are a lot of nettles, but with boot and net they can be trampled to the ground. What looks worse, but is in fact simple, are the tall, rather handsome plants standing shoulder to shoulder. I cannot even tell you their name. Nobody seems to know and I can't identify them in a wild flower book.

They have tall smooth stems, a handsome pale green. The flowers, near the top, are like small orchids in varying shades of pink. They are a cheat. You can snap the stems at any point by the fistful and force them to the ground either right or left to form a serviceable path. What's more, with no effort at all you can keep it open, especially at the river end, so that at dusk you can find your way back.

This rather long description is a self-indulgence: 'It's not difficult to force a pathway through the thick vegetation' would have done, but the five minutes or so it took feed my 'Up the Amazon' fantasy (still in my seventies? Yes, still in my seventies!), but more important to me was the solitary tranquillity ahead, what they once called balm to the soul.

Emerging from the rain forest straight ahead of you across a natural little path was the beginning of another jungle, in fact the beginning of the long narrow island where, many years before, I had spent my seed in honour of the trout. This island was separated from the mainland by a near-stagnant muddy trickle, so it really was an island and in flood time the trickle became a roaring torrent.

Turning right, however, you faced the river. A wonderful screen of trees opposite, and to your right a near lake-size, slow-moving pool, a small rapids and then to your left faster water running down a channel between the opposite bank and a large pebble beach. Then the channel ran into a wider, stiller pool and again espoused the island before running on and out of the wood. Birds ad lib of course. Mink sometimes: pretty little murderous thugs. A heron often clattering up out of the shallows.

Yet what completed the magic of this place was that it proved a certain source of those irrational floods of happiness which are beyond explanation, but, strangely, the heart of it was actually man-made and accidental: a mound of five boulders, a comfortable and convenient throne to sit on, smoke a cigarette (in those days) and listen for the first splash of a rising trout as the sun began to invade the tree-tops.

These stones? They were white, almost marble-like, and not quite natural, as if the work of those sculptors who are let loose in forests to interfere with nature. My son Tom worked it out. Five bags of cement stored there briefly for work in progress. A flash-flood soaking them through and through, bashing them into fortuitous shapes, welding them together. Useless to their owner, they are abandoned. The water strips them of sacking. I think something like this is probably near the truth. Even Noah's Flood would have a problem tumbling them along and leaving them on the same shore, although it's true that for many years in the Home Pool there was a full-size refrigerator (it's still marked 'Fridge Corner' on the map).

So there I sit, on my cement perch, glancing upriver (the Pill Box Pool seems almost insultingly close) and down along the length of Mrs Fist's Island, until they're rising everywhere, and with a dry-fly – it's somehow obviously a dry-fly pool – begin to cast.

*   *   *   *

From the general to the particular. The largest trout, well over three pounds, was caught on a dry fly on the lip of this pool, just before it broke over the shallow riffles. My friend saw it rise and, although concluding from the small rings and the awkward placing that it was small, cast, and was into this huge birthday present. Safely grassed, or at least pebbled, it was a triumphant moment. Our glee, our ridiculous body-language would have convinced any non-angler that we were mentally disturbed.

My friend's name is Matthew. He is the grandson of a famous novelist on one side and Christopher Glenconner, who took me to Scotland, on the other. His mother, too, is a well-known writer, and Matthew himself had an excellent novel published and would like to write full-time. Alas, Cyril Connolly's 'pram in the hall' and other family obligations stand in the way. I relish his quiet narratives, mostly self-deprecating but very funny. He is very shy, too, not good in strange or raucous company.

But take him to a river, and there he becomes, entirely unself-consciously, a kind of Fisher King. I've read that when the Spaniards arrived in South America and rode forth on horses, the natives saw them as centaurs, as Gods. So Matthew by a river. He, his rod, his casting, have a grace, an elegance that make me feel like Caliban. Only David Frusher, manufacturer of luxurious piano stools, is, in my view, his near equal, but with him, admirable as he is, there's a faintly theatrical feel to it. It's almost too perfect. Matthew is as natural as a deer in a clearing.

*　*　*　*　*

That weekend, the weekend of the big trout in the shallows, was like a mad angler's dream. We couldn't go wrong, could cast under impossible bushes, slide down banks with deep pools at the bottom after a big one and find a tiny shelf to stand on. The Usk, the wonderful gypsy, seemed in love with us. Our happiness was palpable.

And then, approximately, a year later, she was out of sorts. Not a fish rose, let alone took. The river, in fair condition, seemed deserted. Fed up after the third day, I suggested a trip to a large stocked pond – at one time it had held the carp for a monastery – to at least to feel again what a fish on the end of a line feels like. We caught our quota of big rainbows; one of mine was five pounds, but, although Matthew was far too good-mannered to say anything, I could tell, as a host, I'd made a serious error. Matthew is a true purist; not one of those who have mugged up the 'correct' attitudes from the Edwardian classicists. He would rather catch *nothing* in a river than Leviathan in still water. I'm much more easy-going, but I would sooner fish with Matthew than anyone else and – it is almost the end of the season as I write – will be joined by Matthew next week!

* * * * *

Half-way down the long wade alongside the island, there used to be a fallen willow, its root still clutching the earth, its branches playing in the current. It was a hostel for trout, and played a major role in the miraculous weekend I shared with Matthew. Then, one spring, it had gone.

During my two decades other favourite features also vanished: a small island in the Home Pool which I could wade out to last thing at night and always harboured trout along its flanks, a large rock above some rapids thereby creating a virtual fish-pond.

Not living at the Tower, never in my life had I expected to be a land-, or in this case water-owner, I wasn't in a position really to keep an eye on things and never knew if Nature or the Water Board was responsible. I was, however, completely prepared to come – 'wading in' is perhaps the appropriate expression – if informed and advised of various threats.

I got a letter, for example, from the very nice man who owned the beat above mine, to warn me that the Water Board proposed to move a whole tongue of stones in order, so they claimed, to modify the flooding. What they failed to mention, but knew perfectly well, was that it would turn a whole long stretch full of our gypsy's twists and turns and backwaters into a straight canal. Boards love straight lines. So do eels, roach, chub, and for all I know barbel and many other coarse fish, but trout *hate* them! A round robin stopped it.

On the other hand I believe the Board was more or less on our side when it came to the major battle – war is perhaps the justified word – in which we and our numerous allies took on the Mayor and Corporation of Newport, and their coffers, to fight their proposal to build a river barrier at the mouth of the Usk, and to create thereby a twelve-mile artificial lake behind it, largely so as to hide the banks of mud during low tide and encourage speculative builders and 'light industry' to yuppify its banks.

The effect ecologically, and especially in relation to the salmon, would have been disastrous, and many scientists, economists and experts in many branches were willing to testify, but the Mayor (hoping perhaps for more than an over-varnished and mediocre portrait to commemorate his mayoralty) was determined to win, had a lot more money to play with than we did, and pressed ahead.

It was fought at our own expense, and it cost a lot, right up to the House of Lords, and for once the 'good guys' won. Recently, en route to Cardiff in a train, I looked out of the window as it crossed the two bridges at Newport, and grinned like the Cheshire Cat at the exposed sea-lion-like flanks of actually rather beautiful mud along both banks.

We have fished now right to the tip of the narrow island and some distance beyond, before a deep shelf prevents further progress. In my earlier Brecon days it was possible to wade across the narrow passage between the island and the shore. This was no longer the case. Mud had built up and within two paces even in breast-waders you were bogged down. It was necessary therefore to turn round and retrace our steps to the point of entry by the cement 'stones'. This was a nuisance and, more in irritation than hope, I often flicked a dry fly across to the far bank and once, on my birthday and an hour before I had to return to London, hooked a large trout, as much to his surprise as mine. (I caught my first

Usk salmon on my birthday too. I liked to pretend they were presents from my father.)

Anyway, as on this occasion I am fishless, I would like to finish our obligatory wade up-river by a final *One Foot in the Grave*-like grumble about the protection of certain fish-eating birds. Our stretch of the Usk, and a lot of the country round is protected, and rightly so, as being of special natural interest, but this extends to two monstrous fowl: the cormorant and the goosander.

For the former, unattractive, even sinister, as I find it, I have a certain sympathy. Within living memory it satisfied its enormous appetite at sea, but overfishing there has attracted it up many rivers and I feel its numbers should be held in check through serious culling. I have noticed, however, that those who 'protect' nature put birds, all birds, very high on the list. It's very difficult to get a culling licence for them, however many fingerlings or salmon parr they gobble up.

Yet while no fan of the cormorant, greasy plumaged bandit that it is, the goosander rates much higher on my list of feathered 'most wanteds'. Not many people know what it is. Here is the dictionary definition: 'Goosander, a sawbill duck of the northern hemisphere.' So? Well, notice its 'sawbill', the equivalent of teeth. It hatches enormous broods too, and its method of fishing (for 'carnivorous' is a word which should have been stressed in its description) is to swim in arrow-head formation along the length of a pool and, diving under like a Busby Berkeley sequence, at synchronised moments to seize, if possible and usually success-fully, a small fish in its sawbill.

This creature looks like an overgrown and untidy mallard. To approach the water and see a great number of them take off (they have white arses) is to experience, in my case, pure hatred. To 'protect' nature is, by definition, to interfere with it. The goosander is overprotected, and while the culling of the alien mink initially aroused my enthusiasm, I'm not sure it hasn't been over-enthusiastic. The escalation of goosander may, in part, be that their eggs and fledgelings have been less threatened because of the diminished number of mink. This reads, I note, like pure fascism. There is, I suppose, a bit of it in most of us. Better to focus it on goosanders than refugees. Better white-arsed ducks than brown-arsed Asiatics.

*   *   *   *   *

We may suppose by now that we are back at the 'stones' and have retraced our steps up the trampled path ('Buffalo, Sahib. See fresh droppings!') and out into the field. What's more, from this moment on I am going to drop this convention of pacing the whole thing out, especially as from now on there are no more pools hiding in woods. Very soon the rest of my water (back to past tenses too) is visible *in toto* most of the time and, while extremely varied, each variation has already been covered. Fish have been caught (and like sex the thrill every time is constant, but repeated description soon palls) at almost every point along the whole length to come, but may be taken, together with the blanks and disappointments, as read unless in some other way remarkable.

One feature of this emergence into an open landscape is that, across the river, is an enormous and steep hill the other side of the valley. Looking up from casting and seeing it is somehow reassuring and I suspect this has a lot to do with a white farmhouse just about half-way up – a tiny doll's house.

12

AS SEEN ON TV

Deftly, admiral, cast your fly
Into the slow deep hover,
Till the wise old trout mistake and die;
Salt are the deeps that cover
The glittering fleets you led,
White is your head.

from *Five Songs* by W. H Auden

Naturally Matthew hasn't been my only fishing guest but, ungrateful as it may seem, I'm not going to fall into the 'Mr Nice Guy' trap of simply listing all those I've fished with whether at their invitation or mine. I do hope I'll be forgiven, but being, if anything, over-inclined to please, I've restrained myself by remembering an aphorism of my father's generation on the theme of 'The three most useless things in the world'. They are:

A man's tits
The Pope's balls
and A vote of thanks for the staff.

It's this last I must be wary of. It doesn't apply, of course, in the case of persons or incidents which adhere, however loosely, to the subject in hand, or which advance the narrative.

An example of what I mean: I had a girlfriend during my 'open marriage' period (she remains amongst my closest personal friends to this day). Being what is known as 'well connected' (i.e. toffs in the immediate family), and what's more very witty and chic, she has spent a fair amount of her life in posh country houses.

During our time together, and especially if there was fishing, she would ask to bring me too, which was very decent of her, as I could prove a bad risk, especially late at night.

In consequence I have cast on great Scottish rivers, over Irish lochs and Southern chalk streams, but while I have many diverting memories of some of these jaunts, they are not more significant, in relation to my fishing history, than a day on a reservoir with a close Welsh chum, or a morning on a North-eastern river with a Geordie jazz-fan. Even so, there were two such invitations which had, in retrospect, a future bearing.

The first was a few days staying with the Earl and Countess of Granville (you'll find no inverse snobbery here). They lived on North Uist, an outer Scottish island, in a modern white house, circular in shape, but with all the windows facing an inner courtyard to defy the winter storms.

Unlike its sister island, South Uist, which is Catholic, North Uist is of the Wee Free persuasion, a severe puritanical sect of whom indeed a representative had refused Diana and me a cup of tea in the early Sixties because it was the Sabbath.

As may be imagined, alcohol is one of the strongest taboos, but happily this had failed to convince the Granvilles. On the contrary they were both partial to a drop of vodka.

Their butler was, it seems, a lay preacher of the Wee Free. I imagine his employers were an invaluable help here; in fact I believe they told us they featured heavily almost every Sunday.

The island has much fine both trout and salmon water and I was looking forward to fishing it, but the weather throughout our stay was so bright, so cloudless and windless, it was impossible and the Granvilles arranged, as a recompense, for us to go sea-fishing.

I hadn't actually fished the sea since we caught all those mackerel off Trearddur Bay, Anglesey, in the Thirties, a monotonous sport even then. Nor had I been impressed by watching sad men on the end of piers. This day, though, was very different.

At first it was just tope, those small shark which become transformed into 'rock salmon' when served in fish and chip shops. Then I was into a large skate. Well, fairly large. There were photographs in the boathouse of locals with skate so big as to overflow a large wheelbarrow (their wings draped over the sides).

What's more, they all feel heavier than they are because they have a trick of bringing their wings forward to form a kind of three-sided box and create a resistance to pressure from the angler. It was a long, hard fight, and a real thrill to look down over the side of the boat and see, for the first time, the great creature beginning to materialise down there in the dark water. I enjoyed it a lot, but thought of it as a one-off. There was no way I could have recognised that skate as a precursor of the big game fish of the Indian Ocean over two decades later.

I left under a cloud. My friend had given me our sandwiches for the trip to look after while she went back to the house to get something, and when she came back I'd eaten every one.

The second significant invitation I've mentioned must wait its place. It will provide yet another proof of my favourite Surrealist tenet – the Certainty of Chance.

*   *   *   *   *

I made two local friends and often invited them to fish with me. Don was a successful builder, fresh-faced and a bit of a boyo, enjoyable company; indeed we often went on pub-crawls together. His friend Martin, smaller and darker, was a truly first-class angler. I don't remember what he did then, but I believe he now runs a private hotel in the West Country.

Both told me early on that as young men they'd done

some poaching. So what, I thought. Indeed, Don now held some piscatorial post in Crickhowell. What they clearly loved was fishing.

*   *   *   *   *

I can only hope by now you have a feel for the gypsy's domain: deep pools, pebble beaches, steep banks, fast-flowing shallows, red-crumbling mini-cliffs at which each winter she nibbles and bites away, waters flowing only through my head.

There is a solitary tree about a hundred yards inland from Mink Island. It looked to me like no other tree I know of in this country, being both smooth and sturdy, not especially tall and with a neat and quite wide umbrella of dark thorny foliage. You passed it if you crossed from one pool to another without following the course of the river. Its likeness nagged at me. Seeing it in silhouette against an orange sunset solved it. It was like a tree of the great African plains (which, much later, I was to visit in reality), the kind of tree that, in photographs, often provides the shade for a pride of lions. Not only in photographs either – on a safari one quite recent New Year, there it was, uprooted from a Welsh valley, replanted in Kenya and under it, grooming, half-asleep, fat on one of the great migrations – THE LION TREE!

On a deep corner Martin hooked and lost a big fish. The next evening, going for it, I took it. Was I pleased? Of course, but mostly because Martin was so good.

There is too a big trout in the pool above Mink Island who

is the escapologist of the sub-aqueous music-hall. His trick was (probably still is) this:

He takes. He seems well hooked. He doesn't fight especially hard. I get the net ready. He's on his side, almost over it, when he rights himself and makes straight for the narrow but deep run up the side of Mink Island called 'Molly's Gutter'. Here he dives down towards a submerged log, wraps the cast round one of the branches and effortlessly breaks it. It happened too often to be coincidence. It was more like James Bond's 'happenstance'. I was asked to contribute to a book of essays called *The One That Got Away* (Merlin, Unwin, 1991). This trout featured in my contribution and I caught him several times after that. Nor am I without a witness. From the Fishing Book:

'Dick Atkins lost a good fish on underwater hazard in Molly's Gutter.

'And that,' as the Editor of *Private Eye* puts it, 'is for the moment (and almost altogether) enough fishing.'

There is, however, a subject which I have never seen discussed in print, but when I brought it up in an after-dinner speech I made at the Fly Fishers' Club (it is the diarrhoeal effect of breast-waders) what *did* surprise me was the number of gentlemen who came up afterwards to confirm my thesis. I feel, too, it's a way to ensure, as we approach the end of this book, that I don't become too nostalgic, that I avoid any tendency to drop a tear on to the page. Nobody, surely, can be nostalgic about diarrhoea.

I would, however, warn all those of a fastidious disposition to skip the next paragraph or two. To avoid offending the scatophobe I've decided to insert in quite large letters the imperative command in public conveniences, 'Now wash your hands', indicating that I've pulled the plug on this discussion.

Naturally, like everyone else, I have had attacks of diarrhoea, some disastrous, but usually I have had few problems in that area. Proportionally, however, the ratio of wader to loosened (indeed completely uncontrollable) bowel movement is beyond the rational.

My father offered me a clue to this theme many years ago which I wondered about, but never thought to pursue. As well as checking the gin bottle in the wader when we went fishing, he also invariably filled a pocket with lavatory paper and quite a large amount at that. This was in itself odd, as his general attitude towards this useful tissue was on the stingy side. Five pieces he claimed were all anyone ever needed – 'two up, two down and a polisher', but he ignored this stricture when he went fishing.

My first practical experience of what we might call 'Walton's Curse' was indeed on the Usk itself and with only a few seconds' warning. I ran into a little wood within view of the Lion Tree, and found as always the accompanying and inevitable law attached to this moment of crisis – nothing will undo. Luckily, however, I had only thigh-waders on, but it was a damn close-, or rather loose-run thing. Given my figure, I found as always the necessary crouch difficult to get right and nettles a frequent hazard.

Now in my fishing life this complaint has often surfaced, frequently in the company of others. There's no question of strolling off, you see. The agitated departure, a kind of loping stagger, makes it obvious what one's about, and it is only that most of my contemporaries have shared this unpleasant experience which makes it just about bearable. On my worst attack of the trots I was, however, alone.

It happened in Devon. The Tower was let and Diana had booked me into a charming old hotel with a rod room, excellent cooking and a strange, completely translucent pale blue lake nearby as well.

I can't say, however, that the West Country is my favourite fishing ground. The valleys tend to be very steep and the fish, while willing to rise, need so instant a strike that I'm always missing them. Still, it was a perfect day, and I'd ordered a taxi to take me to a distant pool and pick me up later, a mile or so downriver. It must have been a Sunday because I'd an *Observer* to read with my lunch, and on this occasion it was that lunch which proved my undoing. I had foolishly forgotten to order it from the hotel the evening before and so was forced to patronise the corner shop. It was a family concern, and with some evidence of in-breeding. I bought a Cornish pasty from a lad with a wandering eye. Then the taxi came. I was wearing breast-waders.

The first attack came half an hour after I'd eaten the pasty (what was its sell-by date? Mafeking night?) I was in a dark wood so it wasn't too bad, and of course I had the *Observer* and bang went the Sports section. However this time and unlike any other attack I'd experienced, this time, and due I'm sure to the age of the pasty (Abdication of Edward VIII? Attlee elected?) it proved multiple; bang went Business, bang went Property, but the worst was reserved for later. I was approaching the gate, the taxi throbbing in the road beyond, when I realised the game was up. This time the wader clips jammed, there was no tree, it was pitch dark – Nemesis had my number. The taxi honking away didn't help either.

It could have been worse. The pants (with prints of fishing flies all over them) took the load. But what to do with them? I shouted I was coming to the taxi and threw the pants as far as I could into a huge plantation of nettles.

The taxi was turning round. Its headlights showed that my proofs of shame were suspended from the branches of a tree, their state fully exposed.

The band, when I told them, were overcome with glee. John Chilton suggested the local police might find them and trace their owner through a laundry mark from our recent visit to Hong Kong.

Always follow Tom's example and take loo paper – and always order hotel lunches.

NOW WASH YOUR HANDS

*   *   *   *   *

They that go down to the sea in ships:
And occupy their business in great waters
These men see the works of the Lord:
And his wonders in the deep

Psalm 107

Accused with some reason of rigid conservatism with a small 'c' (What did I love when I was young? New Orleans jazz, Surrealism and fishing. What do I love now I'm old? Fishing, Surrealism and New Orleans jazz.) Diana has, every now and again, given me a kind of psychic shake.

After Christmas she and Kezzie took to chasing the sun and, in 1995, after my annual and fairly exhausting three-week appearance at Ronnie Scott's, she thought it would do me good to join them.

Even so, knowing I'm happier in foreign parts if I have the excuse of working, she somehow arranged it that I should write a piece about it for the *Evening Standard*, and be sponsored by various interested organisations with no string attached. Actually I loved it. We started off in Nairobi where, thanks to James Fox (the writer, not the actor) we met a charming woman called Petal, who was a child at the time of the Happy Valley murder. Then we went on a lovely safe and comfortable safari on the Masai Mara at Kichwa Tembo (Diana prefers hers rougher with hippos on the dangerous loose and battles between poachers and guards), and finished up at Malindi on the Indian Ocean, where we spent a fortnight at Hemingways, a truly luxurious club with, for those who wanted it, deep-sea fishing attached. The boats, various sizes and prices, bob away some distance out beyond some surrealist rocks. You got to them in rowing boats. You travel over twenty miles to trawl for the monsters of the deep in, at times, quite rough seas and out of sight of land. I wasn't sure how I'd take to it, but I loved it.

The many rods stick out from the boat at every level like a porcupine's quills, and are housed in metal sockets. The bait, bobbing along through the waves at varying distances from the boat, is of strips of fish spliced on to large hooks and covered by pink or other coloured 'ballet-skirts', lowered from further up the line and giving the illusion of prawns or squids.

When a fish takes, the rod in question throws a fit, the Africans make a tremendous high-pitched, adrenalin-flooding din and one of them seizes the rod in question, jerks it vigorously a few times to make sure it's 'home', and transfers it to a master-socket sticking out from the front of a sturdy swivel chair fixed to the deck and where the fisherman now sits, not strapped in, but with a foot-board to strain against, unaware to start with of what's taken the bait and, in my case, initially both exalted and terrified.

As the line on the enormous geared reel was stripped off despite frantic efforts to regain control, as you 'pumped' the rod, hauling it up and then winning a few inches back as you lowered it again, reeling in like mad, it seemed, on that first expedition, not only a long way from the comparatively genteel battle with a brown trout in an English water-meadow, but far from the heavy but unfrantic weight of that Hebridean skate which, in a sense, was responsible for this moment.

Finally, slowly, you win. Not all the fish are huge. On that first expedition my biggest was a 50lb sailfish with its sword like a beak and the huge, rather ragged dorsal fin which gives it its name. Its sensational trick is to leap, several times in a row, right out of the water, an awe-inspiring sight. Unless badly wounded, it, like all the game fish these days, is tagged and released. Only once have they had to kill a sailfish caught by me. It had swallowed the bait right down and even if it was dislodged would have died later.

On that first trip I lost another sailfish and two king-fish, boated a streamlined vulpine barracuda and quite a few of what they call 'minnows' and keep for the kitchen: skipjack, yellowfin, tuna and felusa, some of them extremely beautiful until the colours fade.

Of course I went back in 1998, two years later. This time we stayed, quite a large party of us, at 'Turtle Bay', a friendly place with everything, food and drink, included and rather more adjusted to pockets less capacious than those of the millionaires and rock-stars at 'Hemingways', only a hundred yards up the beach. I wrote a piece on 'Turtle Bay' for the *Express*. It glowed, but then so does *this* brief account, when I am a guest of no one.

For fishing, though, you still have to book through either Hemingways or Ocean Sports, the next club a few more yards up the silver sand. (Did you know this sand is the shit of parrot-fish who live on an exclusive diet of coral?)

This time, in the company of the Ingrams, a father and son from Hampstead, we caught four sailfish, all returned, and, in my case, a not especially big shark, but I went out one more time and hooked and brought to the boat at last the King of Game Fish – a marlin.

Not a very big one, only one hundred and thirty pounds, and they can weigh four hundred and upwards, but quite big enough for me.

To feel the weight and power of this fish is an unbelievable sensation, like rock music played very loud. To be aware it's starting to tire is a mythical experience like killing a dragon to free a chained maiden.

I don't suppose I'll go deep-sea fishing again. It was just in time and I think it will soon be beyond me, but I've done it. That marlin ranks high in this particular old man's encounter with the sea, and I've got 'Hemingways'' diploma to prove it.

* * * * *

I fished on at the Tower until the late nineties! Diana by then did bed and breakfasts most of the time, and many of the parties who came to fish had become not only regulars but friends. By chance, the period when she gave over most of the garden to vegetables, coincided with the miners' strike and she was able to contribute to their food centres. She also arranged for me to do a number of free concerts in the valleys. Seeing the strike at close quarters, actually meeting those involved in fighting for their right to work, gave us a very different angle on foul Mrs Thatcher's 'enemy within'. They lost, of course, and I suppose inevitably. Since that sad day the valleys are turning green again. Somebody could soon write a book called *How Black was my Valley*.

At the height of the strike one of the fighting wives Di was friendly with gave her an orphaned fox cub. It was called James Fox after the author of *White Mischief,* not the actor. James, incidentally, stayed at the Tower quite often over the years and did so at this time too, using it as a base to write one of the few serious, pro-miners articles at the time. His vulpine namesake lived with us until it was essential to reintroduce him carefully back into the wild. In his cub-hood Diana often brought him up to London, where he made his den under a sink in a walk-in cupboard. He would run out and nip me on the bare ankle every time I had to get up for a pee. I never failed to jump!

The big news of this time, however, was when Candy, aka 'Miss Jolly Grin-Grin' of her childhood, gave birth in the Brecon Cottage hospital to a baby girl, originally called Katie, now, by her own decree, Kezzie. As Candy must work, Diana looks after Kezzie a lot. Kezzie has transformed Di's life and is, I feel, the catalyst which at long last has enabled her to come to terms with Patrick's death.

Tom and his partner Lu had a son about two years ago at the time of writing, but Django was too young ever to know the

Tower. Just before the millennium we sold it and moved to Berkshire.

*   *   *   *   *

Why? Because Diana became aware that I was getting to be too old and feeble to handle the Gypsy. The currents, which once caused me no trouble, grabbed me purposefully by the ankles, pushed me here and there against my will. The banks seemed to have become slippier and steeper. Frequently I had to slide down on my bottom. It was time, she thought, for the chalk-stream: the mowed path, the frequent and welcome bench. She began to ask around and almost at once, at a dinner party, the writer Margaret Drabble said that she knew that there would soon be a double-terraced cottage with a big garden on the market as its owners, married doctors, were having to move to Birmingham. Before they'd owned it, it had belonged to the actor Sir Michael Hordern, who always claimed to prefer fishing to the stage, so, from my point of view, it boasted a beneficent ghost. The village, Bagnor, four miles from Newbury, is small and pretty, almost a single row of houses with a pub, The Blackbird, at one end, and a theatre, The Watermill, at the other. We bought it at once, and sold the Tower equally quickly.

When, visiting the Granvilles with my then girlfriend, I hinted that on another occasion she was responsible for an almost unbelievable coincidence, a master-stroke on the part of the

Certainty of Hazard. Here it is.

Back in the Seventies we were doing a concert in a small theatre. My girlfriend said she had a friend close by. We could have tea with him. He turned out to be Billy Wallace, famous in the Fifties as one of the Princess Margaret set. This didn't prejudice me in his favour, on the contrary, but he turned out to be a really sweet and obviously very nice man. He died very young and, despite such a brief acquaintance, I felt really sad. He had a trout-stream in his grounds and, after tea, asked me if I'd like to fish it, but I must put the trout (two as it happened) back.

He was quarrelling with the theatre where we were appearing, on the grounds that people made such a row in the car park and could be heard from his house. Nevertheless he'd booked seats for our performance. This really impressed the management. And the coincidence? Billy lived in Bagnor where I'm writing this book. I can see the theatre from my window. I fish his river.

We moved at the end of the Nineties. In 2000 for the first time I didn't stay at the Tower when I appeared for at least the fourth or fifth time at the great Brecon Jazz Festival, now an international event, once a small local happening. We were there then too – just a piano player, a local band, John Chilton's 'Feetwarmers' and myself. For many years it was organised by the indomitable Liz Elston (she has just retired). My favourite story about her was her need to run round a large table pursued, with lecherous intent, by that also indomitable eighty-year-old jazz-man, the late Slim Gaillard.

It was strange this year to be at Brecon with no home to go to, but I stayed in the beautiful farmhouse of Netty and Simon Harpur. It was, of course, Simon who showed Diana over the Tower all that time ago. A lot of water under the beloved Gypsy's bridges since then.

By chance – no, by the *certainty* of chance – I was to fish the Usk one more time. BBC2 were making an educational series called *Private Passions*, revealing, for example, that the celebrated author and zoologist Desmond Morris is also a long-time Surrealist painter – no news to me, by the way. My contribution was to be fishing. We started, after a minute or two's concert, in a tackle shop in Worcester, full of everything even Eddie Taylor could want, including maggots, not only *au naturel* but green and pink as well. (I once asked a professional match fisherman from Birmingham why he and his fellows were all using pink maggots. 'Just fashion,' he said nonchalantly.)

Anyway after the visit to the shop we went fishing. Where? On my ex-stretch of the Usk: the new owner had not moved in then. David Powell had been affability itself when the TV company asked if they could cross the Great Field with their equipment.

The river was running strongly. I needed an arm to wade in and help establish myself in a good or likely spot. I began to cast and suddenly, against all expectations, was into a big trout.

Mind you, it wasn't the first fish I'd caught on telly. In my view trout are camera-mad, or perhaps I just fish better with a camera on me. Some years before I'd caught a fine TV trout on the

Test – Holy of Holies – but this time! almost certainly my *last* fish on what had been *my* water! Was it my father or the Gypsy who worked it for me? Perhaps both!